Rabindranath Tagore AND GERMANY

Celebrating Gurudev's 150th Birth Anniversary

Rabindranath Tagore AND GERMANY

Dietmar Rothermund
Satinder Kumar Lambah
Martin Kämpchen

Federation of Indo-German Societies in India, New Delhi

Hanns-Seidel-Stiftung, Munich

ALLIED PUBLISHERS PRIVATE LIMITED
New Delhi Mumbai Kolkata Chennai Nagpur
Ahmedabad Bangalore Hyderabad Lucknow

ALLIED PUBLISHERS PRIVATE LIMITED

1/13-14 Asaf Ali Road, **New Delhi**–110002
Ph.: 011-23239001 • E-mail: delhi.books@alliedpublishers.com

47/9 Prag Narain Road, Near Kalyan Bhawan, **Lucknow**–226001
Ph.: 0522-2209942 • E-mail: lko.books@alliedpublishers.com

17 Chittaranjan Avenue, **Kolkata**–700072
Ph.: 033-22129618 • E-mail: cal.books@alliedpublishers.com

15 J.N. Heredia Marg, Ballard Estate, **Mumbai**–400001
Ph.: 022-42126969 • E-mail: mumbai.books@alliedpublishers.com

60 Shiv Sunder Apartments (Ground Floor), Central Bazar Road,
Bajaj Nagar, **Nagpur**–440010
Ph.: 0712-2234210 • E-mail: ngp.books@alliedpublishers.com

F-1 Sun House (First Floor), C.G. Road, Navrangpura,
Ellisbridge P.O., **Ahmedabad**–380006
Ph.: 079-26465916 • E-mail: ahmbd.books@alliedpublishers.com

751 Anna Salai, **Chennai**–600002
Ph.: 044-28523938 • E-mail: chennai.books@alliedpublishers.com

5th Main Road, Gandhinagar, **Bangalore**–560009
Ph.: 080-22262081 • E-mail: bngl.books@alliedpublishers.com

3-2-844/6 & 7 Kachiguda Station Road, **Hyderabad**–500027
Ph.: 040-24619079 • E-mail: hyd.books@alliedpublishers.com

Website: www.alliedpublishers.com

ISBN 978-81-8424-657-5

Published by Sunil Sachdev and printed by Ravi Sachdev at Allied Publishers Private Limited, Printing Division, A-104 Mayapuri Phase II, New Delhi - 110064

This commemorative volume is being published by the Federation of Indo-German Societies in India (FIGS), New Delhi, in association with Hanns-Seidel-Stiftung, Munich, on the occasion of the 150th Birth Anniversary of Gurudev Rabindranath Tagore.

On behalf of FIGS I take this opportunity to thank Prof. Dietmar Rothermund, Satinder Kumar Lambah and Dr. Martin Kämpchen for their contribution to this book.

– Anand Singh Bawa
Honorary Secretary
Federation of Indo-German Societies
in India

New Delhi
4 February, 2011

The Federation of Indo-German Societies in India

The Federation of Indo-German Societies in India (FIGS) was set up over 40 years ago. The principal objects for which it was established are, inter alia:

(i) To strengthen the existing friendly relations between India and the Federal Republic of Germany;

(ii) To promote and develop relations between India and the Federal Republic of Germany in literary, cultural, social, commercial and industrial fields, and explore and develop new areas of mutual cooperation, understanding and goodwill; and

(iii) To help in the organisation of Indo-German Societies in different parts of the country.

Towards these objectives FIGS organises lectures, symposia and get-togethers. Some of these may be focused on a theme, for example, a few years ago a series of lectures on the subject of Indo-German cooperation in science, technology, research and environment was held, and these were recorded in a book entitled *Crossing Borders, Stretching Boundaries*. Some of these are ongoing, like the Wilhelm von Pochhammer Memorial lecture now in its 24th edition. And then, there are lectures and symposia, on a wide range of themes of mutual interest to our two countries.

FIGS has recently arranged the 3rd edition of Pochhammer's *India's Road to Nationhood,* and Gertraude Wilhelm's *In the Kingdom of the Great Moguls* which was displayed at Frankfurt Book Fair 2006.

It runs a scholarship programme for M.Phil and Ph.D. scholars for their research in Germany.

FIGS enjoys the support of the Embassy of the Federal Republic of Germany. Its counterpart, in Germany, is the Deutsch-Indische Gesellschaft.

FIGS also commemorates special events connected with Indo-German relations – the latest being this book, *Rabindranath Tagore and Germany*, published on the occasion of Gurudev's 150th birth anniversary.

To achieve its objectives FIGS has a membership, which consists of major corporates, foundations and eminent academics, amongst others.

Hanns-Seidel-Stiftung

"In the service of democracy, peace and development" is the motto that the Hanns-Seidel-Stiftung applies to its work and mission. The motto applies not only for its commitment in Germany but also abroad.

Former German Federal President Roman Herzog once said "education towards democracy" was the "permanent and real responsibility of political foundations". He stated that this education helped "citizens of an open society to participate in the developmental process of a democracy with as much knowledge as possible".

The understanding of a democracy has to be newly acquired in each generation. Political connections must be made clearly shown – especially to young people. That is the only way to motivate them to take on responsibility and to commit themselves towards democracy.

Besides this conviction effort for our democracy and the free, legal and social order, the fundamental principles and norms of our community have to also be ensured and firmly anchored in the conscience of all citizens. The fast paced and far reaching changes our country is currently facing increase the need for values, for reliable structures and comprehensible order. In other words, the increasing pressure on state and society, economy, science and technology to be innovative makes it even more necessary to remember our historical roots and our intellectual and cultural fundamentals.

Since its establishment in 1967, the Hanns-Seidel-Stiftung has been practicing political education work with the aim of supporting civic education and democratic values in more than forty countries worldwide. The political education work of the organization is based on a human ideal that includes free personality development and autonomy as well as social responsibility and solidarity.

Today, this mission is more important than ever, since requirements for more autonomy, a new "culture of independence" and an "active society of citizens" are increasingly evolving.

Contents

PART -I

RABINDRANATH TAGORE IN GERMANY

A Cross-Section of Contemporary Reports

edited and translated by Dietmar Rothermund

RABINDRANATH TAGORE IN GERMANY

A Cross-Section of Contemporary Reports

edited and translated
by
Dietmar Rothermund

First Edition 1961, published by Max Mueller Bhavan, New Delhi

Reprinted, 2011

PREFACE

I have read with great interest some of the articles included in the Tagore Centenary Volume published by Max Mueller Bhavan, New Delhi. They include contemporary writings on the poet during his visits to Germany in 1921, 1926 and 1930. Many of them are no longer readily available and I have read some of them for the first time. The Max Mueller Bhavan has laid us under a debt of gratitude by bringing together these contemporary records of Tagore's impact on the German mind.

Germany was rising out of the sufferings of the first World War when Tagore visited the country for the first time. In the preceding fifty years, the German people had reached great heights in industrial and military might but had in the process lost some of the spiritual quality which had earlier made Germany the home of philosophy, literature and music. Nationalism began as an assertion of the rights of the people, but almost everywhere it developed an aggressive attitude which sought to deny the same rights to others. Nationalism emerged late in Germany, but perhaps the late arrival itself led to an extreme and unbalanced development. After the colonial exploits of European nations in Asia and Africa in the eighteenth and the nineteenth centuries, they turned against one another and their clash of national self-aggrandizement reached a new climax in the World War of 1914.

Tagore brought to war-torn and weary Europe the message of cultural autonomy and universal brotherhood. He was one of the staunchest supporters of the self-expression of individuals and nations but he also held that their self-expression must not be based on exclusive self interest but contribute to the enrichment of mankind as a whole. The individual can reach his highest development only through co-operation with and service to his fellowmen. Nations can also achieve their true destiny only when they give more than they take from the common heritage of man.

It was not surprising that during his triumphal march through Europe in the early twenties of the century, Tagore should receive the greatest welcome in Germany. Germany had suffered deeply not only materially but also in the spirit and yet an earlier Germany had provided Europe with resplendent gifts of spirituality, intellect and feeling. Bewildered by the experience of the war, German youth found in Tagore the authentic voice of their own glorious heritage and extended to him a warm and immediate welcome that has rarely been given to a visitor from another country.

Forty years have passed since Tagore's first visit to Germany. The predicament of the world has not however changed. In fact, the sense of bewilderment and doom is stronger today in spite of great advances in material prosperity and the prospect of still more astonishing advances. Today, man can plan to explore in safety the outer space but insecurity has entered into his very hearth and home. The threat of uniformity through regimentation is matched by the threat of fragmentation of mankind into petty groups. Never has the message of freedom and dignity of the individual in the context of universal co-operation based on reason been more necessary than today. The world-wide Centenary celebrations in honour of Tagore are a reminder that man has not lost and cannot lose hope but is seeking to find ways of survival and progress in spite of the challenges of atomic destruction posed by blind hatred and narrow self-interest.

I congratulate Max Mueller Bhavan, New Delhi for a fine publication that reminds us of the values of the spirit which alone can prevail over the forces of destruction and darkness.

New Delhi,
21st October 1961.

INTRODUCTION

Rabindranath Tagore visited Germany three times: in 1921 at the age of 60 years, briefly in 1926, and again in 1930. All of these visits were lecture tours which took him to important cities and universities in different parts of Germany.

When the poet first came to Germany in 1921, he was received with great enthusiasm by a large number of people who crowded the lecture halls wherever he went. This first visit was in many ways the most important of his visits to Germany. The early 1920s were a time of intellectual ferment in Germany. The first volume of Spengler's *Decline of the West* had appeared in 1918 and the second volume was published in 1922. The world war had swept away whatever may have been left of the optimism of the enlightenment, and the irrational collapse of a rational world induced many people to look for irrational solutions of irrational problems. The 'cold' intellect was conceived of as an enemy of depth, wisdom, nature and the soul. Genuine heart-searching and wishful thinking were often combined in the contemporary thought of this period. Tagore's message was bound to be evaluated within this frame of reference. He, therefore, found ardent admirers as well as detractors in Germany. His visit was not seen as an irrelevant courtesy call of a foreign celebrity, it was felt to be a contribution to the discussion which was going on in Germany in those days. The statements of the scholars and writers who came into contact with him at that time are not only interesting because of what they tell us about

Tagore, they also illustrate contemporary German thought in its quest for new values and ideals.

Tagore's message of hope and harmony was a consolation after the great war. He was venerated in Germany as a seer and a prophet. His sympathetic understanding and his firm conviction that defeat and loss were but a blessing in disguise encouraged the German people. He attributed his own independent development as a man and a poet to the fact that his family had gone bankrupt. Identifying himself with the fate of Germany he indicated that the defeat and the fall of the old order would give the German nation a chance to start afresh. He hoped that Germany would "make use of the fire that had scorched her for lighting up the path to a great future". However, the fire that had scorched Germany proved to be insufficient, a far greater conflagration was still to come, and we can only hope that our capacity to convert heat into light does not require the test of an even more devastating blaze.

Tagore's message was but a translation of the basic theme of his poetry. His writings are permeated by a mood of longing and expectation. The imagery of waiting and coming, searching and wandering, is ever present in his poems. This mood has a special appeal to the German mind preoccupied as it is with the ideas of becoming and striving. But coming is not becoming and the poet was likely to be misunderstood. Time and space are only dimensions of the separation of God and the soul in Tagore's universe, they are interchangeable parts of a lower level of reality which can be distrupted by the sudden presence of the aim of all longing.

Tagore's affirmation of the life in this world which Albert Schweitzer contrasted with the Indian tradition of the negation of life has to be understood in this context. Tagore sees life as a suspense in the separation from God and he accepts it as such. German idealism also postulated a separation of the soul from God, but here the, suspense was conceived of as motor of evolution. With Tagore, however, the separation was willed by God to create an object of love, and the relationship between God and the soul in this suspense does not give rise to a laborious process of evolution, but it is "Lila", the bitter and sweet tension between union and separation.

There are three ancient ways to perfection: *jnanayoga, karmayoga* and *bhakti;* Tagore chose the latter, but he was very much impressed by what he termed the Western world's perfection of the path of *karmayoga.* His recognition of the validity of *karmayoga* also appealed to the German mind. Work and soul were closely connected in the life of Germany, as Prof. Eucken explained to Tagore, but the link had broken. In the rapid transition from a society based on agriculture and arts and crafts to an industrial society Germany had experienced the painful dissociation of work from its aim, and it dreamed of a restoration of the creative unity of man's endeavour. Tagore was hailed as one who knew about this unity, and who could help to recover it. People often forgot that the poet himself was a seeker; they looked to him for answers which, as they thought, the East had preserved, while the West had lost itself in the material world.

The ideal of a creative unity of man's life and work, the longing for a new humanism was reflected in the German Youth Movement which tried to shed the inhibitions and artificialities of the Victorian age, and propagated a cult of youth and nature. It was this movement which prepared the ground for Tagore's triumph in Germany. The votaries of this movement revived old songs and instruments and roamed through fields and forests. Young and enthusiastic, they felt akin to Tagore's universe, and when he was in their midst they sang and played for him and took him along to the hills and the forest.

The quest for a new humanism also led to a reinterpretation of the old imperial nationalism. Germany has been able to produce the most generous internationalism as well as the most fierce nationalism. Like Indian nationalism German nationalism originally developed under foreign rule—in the Napoleonic era—as a noble concept of national unity and self-determination. But Germany was faced again and again with the problem of territorial unity and integrity in an intricate system of a balance of power. This situation vitiated German nationalism. Nevertheless there has always remained a quest for the redeeming grace of international cooperation. Tagore's message seemed to convey this redeeming grace. In this respect his message is as valid today as ever before.

CHAPTER 1

Sanctified Days with Rabindranath Tagore

Darmstadt, June 10-14, 1921

(Author unknown)

In Darmstadt one evening Tagore was sitting at the window. The setting sun lit his face with its last rays and he relaxed and talked about himself. He told us that his name really means the sun (and he continued that). Often when he was asked to translate his works into English, he had refused to do so and he had said: You do it, you know English much better than I do. His life had been devoted to his people and his own development. But at the age of 50 – about 10 years ago – he had felt suddenly and unexpectedly that he should now, after he had reached his peak, go to the West, as the sun rises in the East and sets in the West. He had begun to translate his works into English, and when he had finished this work, he had to go to the West himself, and therefore he started on his pilgrimage to Europe. Thus the poet and sage of India, of Bengal, became the real poet of our time. the prophet who shows a path to the inner longing of our confused race.

"Tagore is longing personified" – as a Frankfurt newspaper put it so well after his lecture at the university; in political and human dimensions he represents a far-off light.

Every morning at half past ten we met in the garden of the New Palace. We walked on the beautiful lawn which was like a carpet in the midst of wonderful roses under huge old trees, talking to those who shared our hopes and ideas. Then Tagore would appear on the steps of the palace, usually accompanied by Count Keyserling, his faithful interpreter, since he speaks only English. Tagore wears a long, flowing garment. His gait is light and dynamic. Each of his movements is measured and balanced, an expression of quiet dignity. He would come to a few steps which led into the lower part of the garden. People sat on the steps around him, and he answered the questions which they put to him.

On the first morning he told us about the schools in India which are almost all maintained by donations, because every wealthy man feels obliged to accommodate students and teachers in his house. In India culture is not restricted to a small upper class, all cultural treasures are made available to the people. The great poets and bards of the nation go alone or in groups from village to village and sing for the people about the great and the beautiful. The village elders are sages and their main work is to transmit the spiritual heritage. In India – if I have understood Tagore rightly – everybody seems to feel obliged to transmit to others all that he himself has achieved in terms of spiritual values. An Indian never stoops to popularizing a great work of art by bringing it down to a lower level, he retains the original greatness of the work of art and tries to elevate the audience, so that they may enter into the spirit of the work. Perhaps the audience may not understand the work at first, but that does not matter, they feel impressed by the greatness of the work of art and thus acquire the right standards of judgement.

Our cult of the dead seems strange to the people of the East. Cold and lifeless stones seem to be ill-suited to commemorate a man. As an example of how India honours the memory of her dead, Tagore told us about an instance of the commemoration of a man: in a certain place people would gather at the time of the death anniversary of a well - known poet and recite throughout the night the poems of the dead poet, thus honouring his memory – and all this quietly and without much organization, as if it were the most natural thing to do.

Later he spoke about the position of women in society. He compared the European woman with the Indian woman. In India there is an outward restriction and inner freedom, with us there is an apparent outward freedom combined with inner bondage. The woman plays a more important role in India than with us, because there she is the guardian of the personal life of the family. In this circle she rules supreme, and the woman who is expecting the fulfilment of her highest duty is regarded as sacred. The Godhead has two aspects: the one is negative and impersonal, that is will, strength and power – this is the man; the other is positive, personal, female – that is love and sympathy. To the Indian the European women seem to be not free because they have left their own realm and have entered into a completely futile competition with man. With us women venture into a field which is incompatible with their very being, where personality is submerged by outward action. Women can develop only in inner peace, love and sympathy and therefore there is, according to Tagore, no problem of the position of women in society as long as women think of their own mission and task. The respect within the family, the respect for the inherent law of a different being is the one principle on which humanity rests. One little instance of this respect I could see for myself when I watched Tagore's son who is an ardent smoker. He would never smoke a cigarette when his father was present, since his father does not smoke, even if his father would ask him to smoke.

This respect for the other man was illustrated by Tagore's reply to the question whether he believed in a uniform religion. He said: no, and he added that he believed in unity but not in uniformity. Every nation and every man could find his salvation only in his own way, and this very plurality is the foundation of truth, because everything that is incompatible with one's own being is necessarily untrue.

When he spoke about purification, he especially emphasized that this was not a negative but a very positive process, and he compared it to the renewal of nature in spring when there is a new growth and blossoming everywhere. Tagore absolutely rejects any kind of asceticism which does not also set free great, strong and pure forces.

The afternoon of the first day was set aside for the school children. Tagore could not receive them outdoors because the weather was bad, thus they marched past him in the great staircase of the New Palace. He told us about his school in India where there are no walls and fences, no rules and regulations. Whoever wants to jump into the water may jump in and whoever wants to climb a tree may climb it. But the life in this school is very intimate since it is based on unlimited confidence. He said his children did not think him to be an old man, they considered his beard to be but a mask and his hair only dyed grey. He sits among them in the shade of old trees and he has to tell them innumerable stories for hours, and he has to invent games, and in the evening there is a competition among the children as to who can entice him to come to one of the houses when they are going to bed. He would wish that his children could come to Germany and German children to India, because he is sure they would make such good friends. The festivals over there are so wonderful, they are more intimately related to nature. The beginning of spring, of summer and autumn are celebrated, and so is the beginning of the rainy season. The sun and the moon are honoured by special festivals.

In the evening Tagore read some of his poems in the town hall, some in English and some in Bengali. The audience was deeply moved, first of all when he read in Bengali. It was pure music, the hall resounded. It was like the voice of an organ, flowing, without sharp incisions and as if one would play on three manuals simultaneously.

On the next day we listened to his great lecture on "The East and the West". . .. The impact of his words was enormous because he spoke like a prophet with an inner enthusiasm, and at the climax of his speech his voice assumed a tone of sanctity like the voice of a high priest.

On Sunday morning we all attended the great rally on a hill near the town. Thousands had come on this wonderful day of early summer, when the sun glitters in the foliage of the trees, and the forests and the meadows breathe love and life. Here everybody met on the neutral ground of God's pure nature: high and low, rich and poor, old and young, those who were deeply moved and also those who were only curious and looked forward to a sensational event. They went, they sat, they reclined, and on the top of the hill in the midst of the forest stood the lonesome sage. The members of the German Youth Movement sang their songs. Then the Duke of Hesse-Darmstadt who had sat at the feet of Tagore rose and addressed his people ... and asked them to sing a song for Tagore. It is difficult to describe this moment when thousands of voices sang: "Sah ein Knab ein Roeslein stehn"... and the choir was conducted by the Duke, who still lives in the hearts of his people although he is not a ruling prince any more. Song followed after song until the whole assembly spontaneously sang the German national anthem which embodies our own faith in Germany's great future. Tagore appeared to be deeply moved. He could only say a few words ...

The happy crowd surrounded Tagore when he drove down the hill, and the young people with their guitars marched singing in front of and behind his car. The Duke walked with them, and the whole scene looked as if it was taken from the Bible. A quiet walk through the forest gave us time to reconsider what we had gained during this unique day.

A further question which was put to Tagore was: Do you believe in divine justice and how do you explain the insane world war? In this world individuals as well as nations have to fight. Evolution presupposes struggle. However, what kind of struggle should it be? If we indulge in a brutal struggle like animals we lose the higher meaning of life and kill the heart of our life in this way. All wars since the beginning of this world have a material origin. They are never an expression of a spiritual necessity. Passion, craving and exploitation are the true reasons for every war, but they are sub-human. The higher principles of life are self-control and sacrifice. The present longing for peace, however, is aimed only at the preservation of a status quo for the victors so that they can enjoy their success permanently, but this cannot be a true peace. A true peace can never be based on a physical point of view, it can only be based on the spiritual values of self-sacrifice and devotion. Disarmament, the League of Nations, and similar institutions are only an expression of the same old spirit. Power is supposed to be defeated by powerful organizations, this cannot work. A different spiritual attitude is needed, without that there is no hope and no improvement.

We have an example in nature itself. The animals which became more and more enormous, as for instance the Ichtyosaurus, Megalosaurus, Megatherium etc. became finally absurd. They represented a wrong principle. Nature itself could not go beyond this point of brute force. A new principle had to be ushered in. Man was its representative, man who came naked and helpless and without weapons into this world. Man inherited the world and at first proved Christ's word: The peaceful shall inherit the earth. Now we have again arrived at a juncture where further armed combat becomes insane. We cannot solve our problems by force. We must try it in a different way. But we are not yet able to shed the preconceived notions of our past, we are bound by our traditions. We are still striving for our salvation along the lines of the old paths, and we do not yet feel the higher force which alone can be our guide. When man was forced to fight against the animals, he was also compelled to find a higher principle, because he was inferior to them in physical strength. We cannot solve our problems any longer in an arithmetical way by counting our ships and guns, our men and our money. This kind of imperialism has died the same death as those enormous animals: power collapsed in itself. The small, spiritually active entity must become more important than unwieldy power.

India which has been disarmed for centuries, which has been deprived of her external freedom, has retained the God-given power to convert her spiritual power into action. India discovered the higher, spiritual meaning of power. Power became a moral and spiritual weapon, and thus it became the higher principle which will shape the world of tomorrow.

Tagore preached with great inner concentration. Persuasive and super-human in his greatness, he preached the faith in the reality of the moral force. We in the West, says Tagore, believe in the reality of physical force, and this faith –a wrong faith, of course – has given us the strength to get ourselves killed by the millions. But are the Europeans even with regard to their outward circumstances really better off than the Indians who are being beaten up?

The future belongs to the disarmed nations and Christ's word will come true: The peaceful shall inherit the earth.

Some other time he spoke again about his faith in the young generation of whom he expects everything, because their epoch will be one of the greatest of mankind, and he mentioned especially the German youth. As he himself owed his independent development to the bankruptcy of his family, Germany, too, with its present banktruptcy had a chance to start afresh. The German youth was no longer burdened with a past full of narrow prejudices to which it had to adjust itself. No, the German youth has to build its house anew and nobody can prevent it from building this house according to its own requirements. The German youth is holding up an empty bowl, and if its hands are pure, God can pour his blessings into it. And again Tagore showed his love for undiluted truth. Although he was very enthused with the new harmony of German and Indian spiritual life, he did not let himself be carried away, he did not flatter us. He had told us privately that he had never felt so much at home outside India as here in Germany, and because of his intimate contact with his audience, he had been able, for the first time, to deliver his great lecture on the East and the West without referring to his notes. But when he spoke now about the future of mankind, he said that he had met people in London and Paris and in other places, people without claim to fame and renown,no scholars, but people who had nevertheless the divine spark of true humanity within them, and who had made him hope for the renaissance of the world. About Germany he only said that he had found the soul of her people in her forests and her music. I met only a few there, he continued, because only a few can be great leaders, but I felt their power, as if they were millions, and he concluded by saying: Germany has many potentialities of future development.

On the eve of Tagore's departure members of the Youth Movement and students had gathered before the New Palace. The sun was setting, and they were dancing and singing in the midst of a great crowd, while Tagore looked at them from a window. I stayed with some friends a little further in the background in the garden; there, from a distance, everything appeared to be a perfect whole, and the music transformed the scene into a dream. The twilight set in, and at last Tagore had become invisible at his window, but one could feel his presence – he seemed to radiate strength and light. At the end Tagore thanked everybody in a little speech in English. When Count Keyserling wanted to translate his words the whole crowd called out: Don't translate, we have understood everything. This spontaneous understanding was perhaps the greatest homage that the people could pay to Tagore, and he knew it.

The last day was especially impressive. The Duke was so kind as to invite me to be in the palace when the Duncan School performed dances for Tagore. We were all sitting on the broad steps of the palace, Tagore on the lowest step, on a big red cushion. In a side-room music was played and songs were sung in a low voice. The dancers came one by one, barefooted, in their graceful costumes. They approached Tagore and spread roses in front of him until all the marble steps were covered with roses. It was an enchanting sight. The wave of flowers and their fragrance gave us an idea – as if in a dream – of Indian splendour. Then the children danced a dance celebrating the spring, and they accompanied their dance by their songs. The graceful rhythm of these dances impressed Tagore. I watched him because I was sitting directly behind him, and I saw that he was softly clapping his hands, following the rhythm of the dance.

And then came the climax of this week – at least this is how I felt about it. Tagore could meet German workers, could stand in their midst and speak to them. It was very touching indeed to see the great sage among these workers. Although he had to overcome the courtly atmosphere which had surrounded him during all these days in Darmstadt, and in spite of his language difficulties, he impressed them with his warm personality, and his radiating love and the pure humanism which he represented. In absolute silence they listened to his speech, even though Professor Goldstein translated only parts of this speech into German. Tagore told these workers about a sect in India whose members are very poor but who regard themselves as very rich, because they are free from all desire, and because possessions mean only a burden to them which would threaten the peace of their soul. Everything that separates men from each other, all partisan strife is completely incomprehensible to Tagore because of his almost divine love of humanity, and because his values are only spiritual ones. But he is not sentimental, he longs for expression in actions. Tagore continued and said: I am out of place on this platform, I do not know your life, your situation, your problems. I am only a poet. But I would like to live among you in order to give you an insight into the divine love that has made my life rich and meaningful. With these words he broke the ice, and the thanks expressed by the spokesman of the workers ended on this note: that this impression may live on in their minds for ever. Tagore stepped into their midst. He did not speak but they felt his love. Disciplined and respectful they surrounded him and he autographed one of his books for their union library. This was the end of the infinitely rich week with Rabindranath Tagore. These were sanctified days, days of a great experience, days of strength and inspiration. Darmstadt and Tagore have taught me that only active love can set us free, that our true self can only reveal itself in love.

CHAPTER 2

Rabindranath Tagore

Count Hermann Keyserling

"Der Leuchter", 1921-22

On what does the spiritual progress of mankind depend? Most people believe that this progress depends on discoveries of new and hitherto unknown things. It is interesting to note, however, that almost all important thinkers have answered this question by stressing that they have not found anything new – this is true of Confucius, Buddha, Plato and Goethe, and this is true today of Rabindranath Tagore. Nevertheless, these men wbo have laid no claim to original thought have influenced posterity more than all the original thinkers together who were their contemporaries ... Why is Tagore important? As far as the contents of his work are concerned, there is hardly anything new to it. The deepest thinkers expound the same truths at all times. Even if God himself would descend amongst us, he would have nothing new to announce – not at any rate anything that would satisfy our intellectuals. His word would be the word of God only because of its inner meaning that is beyond the human mind. Similarly, the importance of Tagore's message rests entirely on the inner meaning of the old truth which he states. To him it means something totally different from what it means to his critics, because his consciousness is rooted in a deeper level of existence, and thus he can give expression to the working of deeper forces. These forces are beyond the grasp of superficial men, but they express themselves directly through everything that he is and says – this is the secret of his marvellous power over men and nations. He makes thousands of men see once again what all canonical letters have failed to reveal to them. Once the eternal truth becomes directly manifest, it appears to be new and rejuvenating like every force of life which is unique and individual and therefore new. The spiritually new cannot be found on the level of facts but only on the level of meaning. Consequently the final decision does not depend on "What" is expressed but on "Who" expresses it; the abstract content of a thought does not convey a meaning, it is the attitude of the personality expressing it that endows a thought with meaning. We may refer to the theories of Adler and Jung in this connection. If we examine these theories in their more profound context, we understand why men like Buddha, Confucius, Goethe and Tagore, who were no original thinkers in the usual sense of the term, renewed the world of thought, which cannot be said of their more original contemporaries. However, for the very same reason it is rather difficult for the intellectuals to understand these great men. Only those who are perceptive enough to see the inner meaning are able to judge their work.

"Schoepferische Erkenntnis"

... It is not Tagore's intellectual quality nor his talent as a poet which seem to be so very great to me, but it is his depth which is manifest in his life and in his speech. It is manifest because his whole personality is permeated by it from the inner core to the outer shell which conforms not only to the Confucian ideal type according to which wisdom has to express itself in a graceful outward form, but it is also grounded in his detachment and transcendence ... Tagore has, indeed, achieved what he was striving for. Today his transparence is of an absolute quality, and his physical appearance and gracefulness at once convey the depth of his soul, even if he happens to speak about something unimportant.

"Weg zur Vollendung" No.6, 1923,
Keyserling reviews Tagore's autobiography.

The deeper message of this autobiography is that not only our best minds try to transcend the dichotomy of East and West, but that this attempt is also being made by the men of the East, Among Orientals who are interested in the West we usually encounter those who prefer our outward skills to the depth of their homeland. The clan of Tagore, however, has always studied Western thought in the same way as our best minds have studied Oriental thought in order to perfect whatever one's own culture has left underdeveloped and dormant in one's own deeper life. Therefore it was not our knowledge and our technical know-how, but rather our passion which attracted Tagore's attention. In this connection it may be interesting to mention Tagore's article "Vision of Indian History" which appeared in the first issue of his wonderful magazine *Vishwabharati Quarterly* which proposes to build a bridge from East to West. In this article the poet points out that all important things in India have been created not by the Brahmins but by the Kshatriyas, who are the representatives of impassioned action *(rajas).* The appreciation of this fact may explain Rabindranath's bountiful splendour which is unparalleled in India. Although he knows Western culture intimately, he has remained a pure Indian, but seen from the point of view of universality he has attained to a higher level than any of his countrymen before him, because he has to some extent absorbed the predominant features of our culture, too. Thus we may term Tagore the first ecumenical man of Indian nationality, and his importance for all of mankind rests on this fact. This became clear to me when I read his autobiography, and it may also explain why the poet feels compelled to embark ever so often on a missionary journey to all parts of the world.

CHAPTER 3

Hours with Rabindranath Tagore

Paul Natorp

I want to talk to you about Rabindranath Tagore. I feel that the hours which I spent with this wonderful man do not belong to me alone but to all of you, and first of all to those who were looking forward to his visit with us here and who have been disappointed in this hope. I shall try to convey to you all that I can possibly do in such a short lecture. The poet has asked me to tell you how sorry he is for not being able to visit Marburg although he had promised to do so. He was exhausted, and it was time for his return journey; his visit to Vienna was a matter close to his heart, because he had been specially requested to go there. We cannot grudge him this visit, because he did not want to disappoint our German brethren on the Danube.

He wanted to come to Marburg particularly for one reason: he is very much interested in finding out about the attitude of the youth in the most important countries of the West and also in defeated Germany. He wants to come into personal contact with the youth, because the future depends on them. He had been told that I know this youth so well as to be able to inform him about those matters that he wants to know. Therefore he requested me to come to Darmstadt. I gladly accepted his invitation. I have told him the best that I could say. He was very grateful for what I told him and he showed this gratitude by a friendly cordiality with which he received me and which he retained up to the moment of my departure.

What was the motivation for Tagore's long journey to the West, a journey which was not only physically strenuous, but also intellectually and psychologically exacting? I have to say a few words about this, because some rather strange opinions have been voiced with regard to this question. Tagore did not want to be shown around as a poet, sage and a kind of prince, like a fascinating exotic animal. As far as he is concerned, he would rather have preferred to tour all countries as a sanyasi, preaching brotherly love and doing penance. But since he had come to know that for some years past he has been appreciated as a poet and as a thinker in the English speaking world and now also in the German speaking countries, he had hoped to establish better contacts, if he would first tour the West in this capacity.

In this way he hoped to get an insight into the inner constitution of these nations who had only recently hurt each other in bitter enmity and with utmost violence, and who are even now not inclined to show any brotherly feelings towards each other. He considers such a situation to be a permanent and serious threat to human existence, not only to the nations of the West, but also to the nations of Asia and thus also to his own country. He wanted to get a definite idea about the possibilities of bringing about a genuine understanding, not so much among states and powers, which in fact are rather helpless, but among human beings, especially among intellectual leaders (if there are such men) in the most important countries, in the victorious nations as well as in Germany, which has fallen from such a great height. He also wanted to find out what he himself might freely contribute, be it as a poet or as a religious thinker and educator, or simply as the man he is. Tagore as a man is not just the sum total of all his different activities, he is a human being in whom all these capabilities are not separately present, but in whom there may be even more potentialities, and all of them forming an indivisible whole. He did not come to preach an ideology, to excel in oratory or to gather the laurels of a poet, he wanted to extend the hand of a brother, to unite with those who are headed in the same direction, and – if this could be achieved – to form a solid alliance for the common cause of the better future of mankind based on love and simple humanism.

Whoever understood him in this way will be shocked by the fact that Tagore's appearance in Germany has been turned into a stupid sensation of which there are so many, or on the other hand into a political stunt, and this means today in other words somewhat of a public scandal. People have tried to invoke him as a witness to Germany's greatness and as a witness to the enormous injustice which the enemies have perpetrated upon Germany. Some people may have felt that this was spiritually and practically impossible for the Indian, but they in turn criticised the admirers of Tagore for adoring a foreigner. They said that people who believed the foreign Nobel Prize winner to be an imposter nevertheless fell at his feet while Germans who had ten times more merit had not been honoured in this way. Common people, however, as soon as they could approach him (and they could do so in Darmstadt to a certain extent), immediately recognized his unobtrusive human goodness and greatness and greeted him with sincere goodwill.

His last address in Darmstadt was the one to the trade-unionists in the garden of the trade-union hall. He does not have much in common with their party views, but he essentially feels that he belongs to them and they to him, and they freely responded to his love and understanding. People were obviously most impressed by the way in which Tagore received and loved children who also loved him. There was nothing artificial about it, wherever he went he had this immediate contact with children. We know from his poetry the almost feminine tenderness of his understanding of the soul of a child. And therefore I may say that Tagore's encounter with children belongs to the most lasting impressions of the days in Darmstadt. We saw how he talked to them, how they were attracted by him, and how they wept when they had to leave the friendly man. An intelligent boy, who is usually rather critical in his responses, said about Tagore : "I do not know whether he is a holy man, but he is surely a very friendly man." And a little girl explained that one could understand much better what Tagore meant when he spoke in his own language rather than listening to the German translation. All who responded to him at all have had the same impression. When reading the newspaper comments or listening to the discussion of the philistines later on one could not help asking: Has the stupidity of partisan views deprived the Germans of all common sense after they had only recently attained their political maturity; have they lost the ability to see things for themselves, are they unable to see what is right in front of them and what every child can see? This is indeed the sad result of the political infection of heads and hearts: people judge not only by biased standards, once they have adopted them, but they refuse to judge anything at all and simply accept their party-line as a catechism from which they can derive ready-made judgements on each and everything ...

I do not say this only because I want to drive home a point about which I feel very strongly, but because it is vitally connected with my topic. If all the nations into which our poor nation has been split, and the nations of the world in general, have any chance to live together in the future, we shall have to revive first of all the will and the ability to see things unprejudiced and not only through partisan eyes. Otherwise, even if gods may descend on earth ... it would be all in vain, the gods would be voted down by majority vote. But why do I speak of gods. Man is of no value to man any longer, nor is he of any value to himself, as long as the party decide everything.

Rabindranath Tagore, however, is a miracle man to us because he has succeeded in remaining a man in the midst of the 20th century and he is still a man in his sixtieth year. He knows how to meet men in a human way, whatever their behaviour may be, he is at his best with children. But after all there is a child in everyone of us, and he knows how to appeal to this child in us, because he himself has remained a child at heart, an uninhibited human being, while others try hard to become old men and women and conceal the child within themselves.

I think we are now getting at the core of this miracle man. Why does he move us in such a way that one cannot resist him? It has been said that he has a miraculous charm: that he is "irresistible". But he who has seen him feels that these are not the right attributes. A child that has not yet learned to repeat stock phrases does not say this uncle is charming, he says he is good and loving. He loves him without asking questions. But, why? I think because Tagore sees in every man unconditionally the human being and looks to the root of his human existence, he knows how to get at the indestructible nucleus of human existence. Here I find similarities with the best in Quakerism. I read a small booklet by Rufus Jones who describes the 'passion' of Christian love as the recognition of the value of every single human being, the divine potentialities, the royal destiny of every man, that offers a community even to the lowly and lost, embracing everybody. Similar passages can be found in Tagore's work, but with him it is not a doctrine, passion or religion, it does not need these labels, it simply exists. Wherever it is so there is no struggle between brothers and all the conflict within one's own soul ceases, man is reconciled with man, he is reconciled with nature and with the origin of all creation which is revealed to man in the only true source of revelation, his own soul. Wherever this does not exist, the most dramatic poetry, the most convincing doctrine, the most intense religious revival and the most burning pain of self-sacrifice or even martyrdom will be of no avail, man runs amuck in his hatred and what is worse than hatred in cold estrangement from others and from himself, he murders mankind in himself and around himself; he kills nature and he would, if he could do so, even kill God in nature and in himself. Of course, the God in us cannot be killed. But in a similar way as in the cruel war the bodies of many of our brethren lay buried under tons of earth and could still be rescued if brotherly love took care of them, God today is submerged though not dead and he can be liberated in us only by brotherly love. This is the simple and deep faith to which Rabindranath Tagore is a witness, a faith about which we do not hear much these days. And for this reason the unprejudiced mind feels immediately attracted to Tagore.

One can never forget how Tagore stood in the wonderful forest on the Herrgottsberg near Darmstadt and how he talked to the crowd around him in simple and friendly words, and how the crowd responded to him by singing German folksongs which he very much liked to hear. I was with my wife among the crowd. A simple old man asked for an explanation of what Tagore had just said. He listened and nodded and finally said, "He must be a man with a strong faith." We answered: "Yes, indeed, he is a man with a strong faith, he believes not only in God but also in man." What did Tagore say? He said something like this: As the forest grows and rises out of the dust of the earth and stretches its arms towards the light of the sky and bears foliage and fruit in gratitude for this liberation, thus the song arises out of the soul which is pressed into the dust and reaches, in jubilant liberation, the throne of God. – You may say that these words are not very extraordinary, that anyone of us could have said the same thing. Perhaps – but the way in which he said it made it appear especially meaningful to all of us, it complied with Goethe's definition of the term meaningful: it meant much to the speaker and therefore it also meant much to the listeners. It meant in other words: Here in the German forest, in German songs, in the midst of a friendly and understanding crowd on a sunny Sunday afternoon you experience something of what you have been looking for; you have an insight into the German soul that greets your Indian soul and accepts your greetings. May our souls from now on grow up together in freedom, equality and fraternity like the dark and beautiful trees of the forest which reach out for the eternal light.

Tagore's speeches were always simple, like his poetry, they could be understood by every simple man, woman or child and remained unintelligible only to the super-wise, the learned scholars and Pharisees. But each of his words was meaningful and even the obvious always arose from the depth of the experience of the moment. He always summed up his innermost insights. It was touching to see how he would step aside for a short while at the conclusion of a serious discussion, meditating for a moment on the result of the discussion, as if in prayer, and then turning back in order to say good bye, shaking hands and looking at you with an intensity as lovers might look at each other after their first meeting. The sums of all things are always simple. Tagore never bothered to go into details and calculations in his speeches like those we are used to listen to in the speeches of our orators (which therefore seem to be so cold). He always spoke in terms of sums and therefore every sentence seemed to be obvious and simple. And yet, when he finally came to the sum of all sums, we were confronted, all of a sudden, with something great and new. It is not surprising to hear that this man always gets up before sunrise and that he spends the early hours of the day in solitary meditation immersed in an inner vision and silent prayer. At that time he may attain to the sum of sums which remains with him throughout the day, therefore his utterances which appear like momentary flashes of insight do not vanish as the moment vanishes but get into one's mind and do not fade away.

This is probably the reason for Tagore's fame as an educator. He exercises his educative influence through his poetry and his writings, but most of all through his school at Shantiniketan; and he influences not only thousands of people directly, but also the millions of Bengalis whom he has infused with a national spirit. This is an achievement without a parallel in our time, and so far as the West is concerned, we would have to go back through the history of many centuries in order to find a similar phenomenon. This fact distinguishes Tagore from all others with whom we could compare him as a poet, as a sage, as a revivalist and as a leader and educator. Such men usually gather a community, perhaps in the manner of the pied piper. But there are so many pied pipers and everyone of them has to preach something new in order to attract people. Finally everyone talks to himself only and draws a narrow circle around himself... and thus all speech-making and preaching does not unify people but separates them and makes them cold and indifferent. Words, sounds, even paintings produce a loud noise like bombs that are thrust at us, they tear holes and it is as if hot lava pours out of wounded souls. But this lava only burns and buries all that comes into its way. There is no communication, no revelation, people hide as if behind a barbed wire. Intellectually and spiritually we still live in the trenches of the last war, and we have forgotten that there is a wonderful and great world full of the joy of peace and creation beyond this barbed wire.

This brings us to the question: What can Rabindranath Tagore give us? What can the East give to the West? But before I speak about the contents of his speeches, let me speak about something else which is closely connected with what I have said before. I want to speak about the form and style of his recitations and lectures. It takes some courage to speak about this subject because I have to say certain things which may appear to you as exaggerations. What impressed me most in Tagore was the enormously high level of form and style of this cultured man which contrasted with our lack of all these qualities. I do not want to criticize the manner in which the poet was introduced to us and the way in which his speeches were interpreted. We have to be grateful to those who arranged this meeting. But one could not help feeling how little the arrangements corresponded to the spirit of the Indian. It was an example of the inner cultural conflict between East and West. One could feel something of that spirit of violence of which none of us can claim to be entirely free. I hope the Indian in his understanding sympathy did not see in this anything else but a symptom of the wounds which we received in the war – not only in the war of those terrible four years, but in the war which had started long before, and which is still continuing and growing in its vigour and which may grow even more until it becomes unbearable.

The violence, this recognition of an impending danger which threatens not only the West, but which also threatens more and more the holy peace of the East, has been on Tagore's mind for a long time. He had to be prepared for finding this violence here with us and with all the nations of the West. He expressed this in some of his poems which came to us from afar during the war. His journey was a martyrdom because he had to witness here the stark reality of all that which he could only surmise when he was still at home. He is not a monk who has renounced the world but a man who loves this world and all human beings, who responds to all human values and who is therefore very sensitive when he sees the desecration of everything holy. He must be indeed very much hurt by all the experiences which do not agree with his own pure, strong and noble life. He told us so again and again, not by way of a complaint or an accusation, and also not in a tone of soft forgiveness, but rather in a prophetic manner, stressing that the salvation had to come from among ourselves, and that he was confident that there were signs of improvement and not the least here in Germany.

His eyes were shining when I told him: Yes, there is a new spirit in our youth, there is a new growth, and whenever one cares to listen and to look carefully, one can see a deep seriousness, a pure and courageous spirit of action which is derived from the innocence and openness of genuine youth, a spirit which we had missed for a long time. I reminded him of his little humorous and harmonious play "The Cycle of Spring" which nevertheless conveys such an important message. He had written this play for the boys at Shantiniketan and he himself had played the role of the poet. This is the story: The boys are celebrating the beginning of spring and they want a new play. The poet improvises one. They should go and find the "old man" of whom everybody talks, but whom nobody has seen. They start in the morning and search for him throughout the day. Late at night they find his tracks and they think: when we find him we shall punish him . The tracks lead into a dark cave, they are sure to get him there. But when they catch him at daybreak and he steps out of the cave they discover that he is not an "old man" but their beloved master. They see that ageing does not really exist, and that what appeared to be aging was only a process of rejuvenation, as the day is born out of the darkness of the night, and that which is in the way of this rejuvenation is easily left behind. Truly a simple plot, which, as the poet gladly confessed, "he had stolen from the lyrical drama of the poet of this world". I dared to tell the poet that this play sounded in every detail like a manifestation of the spirit of the German Youth Movement. For this reason I could not but feel hopeful about the fate of our people; it will find itself again in this youth, it will pursue the "old man" until he reveals himself as the eternally young, the symbol of rejuvenation. Tagore's eyes were shining! And they were shining again when on the occasion of the last open meeting, in the garden of the Duke, one of our youths thanked Tagore (in English) and did so in a similar way as I had done in our private dialogue some days ago; he also mentioned the "The Cycle of Spring" and applied this parable to the wonderful old man with his childlike eyes who was standing there in front of us in royal dignity.

Indeed, one has to have the indestructible soul of a child and virile strength in order to retain the courage of faith in these days, and thus not only to preserve but to enhance what I had praised in this man: form, style and culture. Actually I am looking for a more precise term for this phenomenon. Perhaps I shall get closer to what I want to express by first mentioning what it is not: it is not something that can be learned, trained, or bred, even though much education and discipline may be an additional requirement. It is nothing that can be made, it is something that grows, that rises from hidden sources like the growth of a tree, or a forest, of a landscape, of the earth as a whole, of all the infinite family of planets and suns which together are our living world, the living body of God: growth emerging from the right kind of soil with sufficient space and time, enough of light and breath of the sky, the very essence of harmony, rhythm and '*melos*' of growth, rising from the earth but striving towards the sky. But all this is nature, not culture, you may object. Of course, no comparison is perfect. There is, indeed, a difference: The tree – at least that is the way we think it to be – does not know about its growth, it simply grows. Man knows about his growth, he enjoys it, clings to it and forms it with his will and he radiates this growth and encourages others to free, equal and brotherly growth around him. He helps them to grow, and when the time has come, he freely yields, so that others may take his place. This is culture and yet remains nature, only it is elevated to a new dimension of consciousness. This is the foundation of form and style.

Some people have coined the term culture of expression. I think this term to be a tautology. All culture is expression, language, self-expression, giving of oneself to others in order to find oneself again, a greeting from one to the other, like breathing in and breathing out – Goethe compared it to the two phases of the heart beat. This is the origin of verse and melody, through contrast harmony is deepened and reveals its connection with the eternal and infinite harmony of the universe of which we are unconsciously aware and to which we always return, it is rhythm in its most all-embracing meaning which also includes all works of art. But art is again a rather insufficient term; the Greek culture did not know this term, because '*techne*' meant to them only the technique, the way of doing something. Even less sufficient is the term aesthetics which seems to imply that we are aiming at the nicety of outward performance only, as if we are not interested in the formative, dynamic and pure qualities of growth. This growth, of course, rests blissfully in itself. But it is only the creative energy (the 'Poietic') which decides whether any substance arises out of this bliss. He who does not create a form does not really have a feeling for it. It is not something beyond life that thus finds expression, but it is life itself and its perfection which expresses itself in this way: growth, gesture, the movement of the muscles and nerves become word, sound, line and bodily form, alive and vibrant, never stiff and dead.

What I admired most in Rabindranath Tagore was the marvellous unity of expression, his wonderful poise – not a single movement of his limbs, of his sensitive hands, of the muscles on his forehead, of his mouth ever disturbed the complete harmony of the expression of his inner self. The soft, almost feminine modulation of this voice and the royal dignity of his appearance enabled him to express the infinite range of sentiments from sweetest wisdom to the most tragic mood. Let me try to illustrate this by a few examples. Even the recital of some poems in English, which I had never heard in this way before, was impressive because of its vibrant and rich tone. We know that good orators are able to portray the wind and the falling of the rain as well as the rolling thunder by means of their expressive modulation; but with Tagore all this was even more pronounced and heightened. The words themselves were falling, raining, thundering, and made the soul resound. When he recited one of his most beautiful poems:

"He comes, comes, ever comes", there was a tense, anxious but still infinitely blissful longing for something that is unheard of, overwhelmingly holy. He who recited the poem seemed to express in every single word the whole theme of the poem which was embedded in his soul; and the completeness of the poem seemed to arise in him only here and now like a bud that opens when it is touched by the rays of the sun. But all this became insignificant when compared with the subsequent recital of the same poem in the poet's mother tongue. There was not only a greater freshness and originality, there was also an even subtler rhythm, a finer variety of sound and response, and a wonderful melody which hardly any language of the West can attain. Only if we go back to the rhythm of ancient Greek music or to the best compositions of German music, we may get an idea of the possibility of such a music of language. But even then we shall have to confess that we have never listened to anything that can be compared with this music. There is much that seems to remind us of Greek music, but the alternating short and long tones are not so important in this recitation as the recurrence of short and long tones of equal length in a three beat rhythm, the measurement without ever being rigid seemed to be nevertheless very accurate as we expect it to be in real music but hardly in a recitation of poetry. But this recitation was not a song, it was only a rhythmic diction with an accurate and subtle intonation. I think that listening to this I became, for the first time, aware of the importance of the smallest intervals (not only quarter notes but an eighth of a note). There was a poem which required a slight raising of the voice from one verse to the next. This was achieved within the narrowest perceptible limits but with an audible accuracy. Thus it went on from one line to the next. But if indeed an interval of one full note or a half note occurred (the whole poem encompassed hardly more than an interval of two full notes, let us say from b to d) the effect was as if in our music a whole octave had been covered.

The most impressive, however, was the recitation of some verses from the Vedas in Sanskrit; Tagore wanted to demonstrate how the rhythm of modern Bengali was based on the old holy scriptures and that it has essentially remained the same throughout. Indeed, both these languages are very similar, only the old language is by far richer and greater, in its effective contrasts and wonderful harmonies it is solemn and majestic. We do not find a trace of hard and fast rules, there is a wonderful freedom which nevertheless implies the greatest unity to an extent which is known to our music only at its very best. I do not know how all of this is related to the vocal and instrumental music of ancient and modern India. I have read about it that even the men of the East need many years of preparatory study for it. The few samples of the recital of poetry which are only half music give an impression of a profound art. And Tagore himself is a composer, singer and musician; he composes the accompaniment for his poems.

These were the highlights. But even in the everyday language of discussion and conversation (in English) which had nothing to do with poetry and music, he showed a similar subtlety of rhythm and intonation of word and sentence, of intervals and facial expressions. When listening to somebody else his hands would slightly move as if they wanted to express the reception of the other's words. Everything in this man speaks, the whole man speaks: he himself is the living expression, the living word. He did not learn to be like that, he did not plan it or train himself to behave like this, it is so deeply connected with the essence of his being that it could not be anything else than this. It has grown, it is not made or affected. And this is what I want to call culture. Up to now I have not even mentioned the most wonderful element of this amazing language: the expressiveness of his eyes, these eyes, which – if anything in this world could make a poet out of me – would make me a poet.

I am not in the habit of deifying human beings, however great they may appear to be. But I must say: if there are more of such Tagores in India (and people say there are) I can understand what I was hitherto unable to understand: how Indians are able to see gods in men who are living amongst them. The Indians see in such men gods who lift them up from the dust and raise them to the heights of purity where they can approach the godhead, and thus they learn to honour God in themselves.

We have forgotten about this. Tagore expresses surprise in his book "Sadhana" about the fact that the Christians although they know about the commandment "Be perfect as thy father is perfect", consider it to be a blasphemy when one ascribes perfection to a human being. He himself does not want to be a god, a saviour, a prophet or a holy man. Those who assume that he does not know about earthly passions and that he does not recognize them as a poet, do not know him at all. But he believes it to be the truth when in his play "The King of the Dark Chamber" the king answers Sudarshana's question: "What do you see?" in these words: "I see that the darkness of the infinite heavens whirled into life and being by the power of my love, has drawn the light of a myriad stars into itself, and incarnated itself in a form of flesh and blood. And in that form, what aeons of thought and striving, untold yearnings of limitless skies, the countless gifts of unnumbered seasons!"

Thus the poet sees the divine in the soul of man, in every pure relationship between man and man, man and woman, mother and child. A poem in the book "The Crescent Moon" tells us : "Heaven's first darling, twin-born with the morning light, you have floated down the stream of the world's life, and at last you have stranded on my heart. As I gaze on your face, mystery overwhelms me; you who belong to all have become mine. For fear of losing you I hold you tight to my breast. What magic has snared the world's treasure in these slender arms of mine?" In this way the Indian feels the divine quality of a mother's love. My wife asked Rabindranath's son, who accompanied him on the journey, and who does not have the same high spiritual qualities as his father, but who is nevertheless a genuine and lovable man, whether the poems of children which she likes very much had referred to Tagore's own family. He bashfully admitted this but added that they did not refer to him but to his brother who had died young. My wife said with a tone of pity: "You have also lost your mother early". "Yes", he replied, and he closed his eyes as if to recall his mother clearly, and then he continued, "when I was 13 years old."

The German people were once justly praised for the high regard in which they held womanhood and motherhood, which they considered to be almost holy. Even during the last war many of the dying soldiers cried out for their mother. But where is all of this today? ... Tagore does not know all about our cities and industrial areas, our blackmarketeers, our cliques of writers and artists. He restricted himself to positive remarks about the advantages of the East, where the working power of women is not so shamelessly exploited for profit as with us, where women are not yet as alienated from their life as mothers and from their duties in the home. And therefore women are still venerated in the East as they used to be in our country. Whosoever speaks of reconstruction should realize one important fact: a nation that does not respect mothers, that does not want mothers, will perish because it wants to perish.

Our appreciation of nature which had once been so strong in the German nation disappeared in the same way ... The Indian, however, still loves his native soil. In a voice charged with emotion Tagore told us that once somewhere in India a commercial firm wanted to drive the peasants from their soil in order to construct a plant. But the peasants did not leave their land, and covering it with their bodies, they even stayed on when the brutal messengers of culture poured hot water on them. They preferred to die rather than consent to give up their land for usurious profit. In Germany you cannot witness such love of the soil and of the country any longer ... the people only look to money and entertainment in the exquisite fresh air of the industrial towns and in cinemas and tobacco shops ... is this our much praised culture which we want to give to the poor, backward inhabitants of the "ancient continents"? This would be the end. Whatever we may destroy here at home will be after all only the impressive debris of something that was a culture once upon a time. And perhaps it is necessary to get rid even of these remnants in order to build a new and more genuine culture on a fresh foundation. But in the East there is still a living, unimpaired culture, and this culture may be spoiled and uprooted. This culture has still its natural roots from which it draws sap to nurture such blossoms and fruits as this

Indian shows them in his works, in his very being and he is only one among many others. This is to me the most important significance of his visit to the West. This is the message not only of his spoken word, but of his very appearance in the midst of a world which has lost its integrity to an alarming extent, which is going to pieces and which wages a suicidal war against all genuine culture. For this reason I was so deeply impressed with the culture of this only typical Oriental whom I happen to know. And this is also the essence of his mission. There was nothing surprisingly new in what he told us. Being experts in all sciences, we know all that he could have told us for centuries: and if we think in our Western way that this man has come only to lecture to us about his knowledge of East and West, then we might have held up our chin and said: You could have stayed at home, you could have saved yourself the torture of touring the deserts of the West, because whatever you may tell us, we know it and we know it more accurately than you do. But this does not apply. Tagore is not a professor of comparative ethnology on a lecture tour, he is a man, he represents the urgent call of the wounded, but still unimpaired soul of the East. He calls for our own soul. He is looking for that point of unity where the souls of the East and the West can meet. He searches for the god of whom Goethe said: "To God belongs the Orient, to God belongs the Occident." It is a call of painful longing that is nevertheless imbued with an ardent hope that is greater than all fear and hesitation. He comes, comes, ever comes! This is not science, this is consciousness. It does not rely upon the calculations of reason, but rests on an inner faith. It does not know proof or evidence, it only knows the appeal for a quest in our own soul. A contact between soul and soul must be established; here the spark will come off which will re-kindle the great flames of the divine love that unifies all.

Of course, Tagore also asks for the reasons for the enormous difference between the East and the West. He likes to deduce this difference from the experience of the forests which the Aryans encountered in India and in which they lived in close communication with nature, thus being free from the necessity of a struggle for existence which faced their brethren who had gone westward and who had to make a living on the high seas or in fortified cities. Thus their chief characteristics were formed by the struggle against nature in which they saw more of an enemy than of a mother. He points out the differences of climate which also generated a different fauna and flora in East and West. Of course, such differences cannot be overcome. But they need not be decisive. Provided that there is some goodwill, a balance of advantages and disadvantages could be achieved among nations. But why is there a lack of this goodwill? Tagore does not deny the inevitability of differentiation and of a struggle of elements which are mutually opposed to each other. He does not dream of a human existence in some lost paradise of innocence and simplicity. Whatever there is, had to be necessarily so. Differentiation also meant an increasing utilisation of all potentialities of life, invention, technology, organisation of working together and fighting together ... But this also implies a race away from the centre of all things towards the periphery. The centrifugal forces are increasing. Everything is subdivided more and more. Wars are fought not in order to defend essential things, but only in order to amass more power, more space for new activities without rhyme or reason. The body which was supposed to serve the soul, compels the soul to serve it, and it would kill the soul if the soul could be killed.

Fortunately the soul lives and cannot be killed. But it is being tortured and humiliated... The real destiny of the soul is to penetrate the universe and to be imbued with the universe. It is wrong to assume that according to Tagore or according to the views of the Indians or Orientals in general, man has to renounce the world and the splendour of this life. The much quoted Nirvana only implies the overcoming of those vices, which do not liberate the soul but hold it in bondage ...

In nobler human beings the new man has already been incarnated, the man who has God in his soul, the man who is weak and helpless compared with those who still consider themselves to be powerful and great today, although nobody really enjoys pure violence any longer or seriously believes in its efficacy. However, this does not mean that will and intellect should henceforth abdicate their functions, but they should know their limits and willingly serve the noble qualities of the soul. I have only one final question: whether we, the German people, shall be able to make our own contribution to this new age, the era of the soul? Tagore emphasized that to him all leading nations of the West seemed to be equally threatened by the same errors and perils. We had thought that this did not apply to us, at least we did not want it to come about ... Who wanted it? Did we all not run into it blindly? After having lost a sense of proportion, we challenged the whole world without even realizing it, and after having done so, we had to fight up to the bitter end. And the spirit of fighting has not left us yet, this spirit is an obstacle to the new spirit which is moving us now more deeply (so we think) than it does the other nations. But the spirit is there and we can hope that according to our national character it will grow stronger and stronger within us. The outward defeat which is such a great burden to us, is also an asset because it demonstrates the futility of a mere striving for power, the second age of the dinosaur, of which Tagore spoke. Tagore told the workers in Darmstadt, while referring to the class struggle, that the salvation always comes from the oppressed and never from the oppressors. The history of our nation proves this point: whenever we had to bend under a cruel yoke, we reached our greatest heights ...

Let me sum up my impression. Tagore is not a saviour or a holy man to us, no apostle and reformer, no philosopher or ethnologist, and not even an educator, although we are greatly in need of one these days. He himself has emphasized that each nation can only create its own indigenous religion, poetry and culture by using its own and not alien resources. He does not want to convert the West to the religion and culture of the East or vice versa. He wants that East and West should cooperate in order to save the afflicted humanity. In this way he sets a great example for us, an example that we should not imitate blindly, but that we should emulate in our own way. He warns us in a brotherly spirit. He does not force his criticism upon us, he wants to help us to see the danger and to overcome it. He gives us hope and consolation, he demonstrates to us in his own being and work the integrity and profundity of genuine humanity, and thus he shows us that after all mankind is not living in hell, estranged from all that is divine, without love and soul. We thank him for this as brothers and friends. We thank him who has come to us as a brother and who remains close to us even though he may be far away.

CHAPTER 4

Tagore's Arrival in Berlin

Helmuth von Glasenapp

Deutsche Allgemeine Zeitung, May 30, 1921

(Glasenapp met Tagore on his arrival and reported about his conversation)

The poet told me that he was very glad to be able to visit Germany at this time. He was sorry that he could not come to Germany last year due to some passport difficulties created by some foreign authorities. Germany means to him not only the country of poets and thinkers, the country of Goethe and Kant, but first of all the country which has shown an unselfish interest in the study of Indian languages and religions. He quoted Heine who had said that the German nation had been the only one that did not try to capture outward treasures in India but had striven for the spiritual values of India. Tagore hopes that German and Indian minds will be able to cooperate in order to bring about a better understanding between the East and the West. In working for this aim which still seems to be rather remote, Tagore is planning to convert his school at Shantiniketan into an international university which should promote the idea of a reconciliation of all nations and a unification of the cultures of the Orient and the Occident ... Long after Tagore will have left Germany, the ideas for which he stands will remain with us and he will also have pleasant memories of his visit to Germany.

CHAPTER 5

Tagore in Berlin

Max Hochdorf

Vorwaerts, Berlin, June, 1921

Berlin University wanted to receive Tagore in a festive manner. But about noon at the time which had been fixed for the poet's lecture, the students stormed impatiently into the great assembly hall. The vice-chancellor and the professors were surprised and annoyed at the curiosity of the youth which knew no bounds. They were afraid of a veritable riot which would have ill-suited the reception of this herald of meditation and wisdom. The vice-chancellor requested the students not to violate the dignity of the university ... he threatened to call in the police if his request was not heeded. The turmoil subsided only after some time and Policemen had to clear the way for Tagore so that he could reach the rostrum.

He is a lean man of medium height. The oval bronze head is surrounded by a well groomed silvery beard. The face has a mild appearance; with his long moustache and well-cut beard he gives the impression of a fit and healthy old man. Tagore's body is concealed by the long grey silk gown of the oriental priest, but he does not seem to be a strange and aloof prophet. The priestly gown seems to be with him an official uniform. Perhaps he would feel uncomfortable in European clothes. I tried to catch a glimpse of his eyes. They are hidden under deep eyelids. While the vice-chancellor welcomed the respected guest, he himself seemed to be preoccupied, he did not take notice of the fact that these remarks were meant for him. He leafed through the pages of the typewritten manuscript from which he was soon to read his treatise on the ideals of his country.

Yes, indeed, he read a well-prepared lecture with well-enunciated points, carefully divided into paragraphs. He did not think of delivering a fiery speech inspired by an orphic mood of momentary exultation. His voice is surprisingly high. He lapses into a certain monotony, because he carefully follows each and every sentence of his manuscript. He uses no gestures to emphasize the different points of his learned treatise. Only when he quotes a Sanskrit verse he raises his voice in a singing tone. Only then he becomes rhapsodic and looks up from his manuscript, and when he gives the English translation of these quotes he tries to give a similar expression to these words. From the singing falsetto of the quotes he lapses back into the European intonation, and he says: The Himalaya is holy, the mountains and the rivers are holy, the animals and birds are holy, and man is holy, the laughing of animals and men is holy ...

This was the essence of what he wanted to say at Berlin University. In Indian wisdom and in the religious and philosophical writings of ancient times, as well as in the imagination of Kalidasa, it is the unity of mankind which is the aim and the meaning of the song. Man should not be torn by conflicts, but he should conquer the world by conquering himself. Passion subsides because it does not have any access to man. All the parables that Indian thought might offer to the learned and to the simple-minded are always aimed in this direction.

After the lecture was over Tagore was surrounded by professors, ministers and diplomats and Indians in white gowns and brown turbans. Everyone wanted to meet the celebrated man. Although he is not very tall, he bent down to everybody who asked him a question. And again I could not see his eyes, and I could hardly hear his voice because in a dialogue he speaks in a subdued, intimate voice ... The place between the opera house and the old library was brimming with crowds. Even the newspaper vendors left their stands in order to come and see. The students and all the working people who had found some free time in their lunch hour were waiting for this man whom they consider to be a wonderful enigma. If they could have penetrated this enigma, they might perhaps have found that hidden behind this beautiful and venerable forehead there existed a world of confusing ideas which a good European of this year 1921 may have to reject. But it was a festive day for Tagore; let us talk about these dangerous matters some other time.

CHAPTER 6

Preface to 'Rabindranath Tagore's Faith'

Rudolf Otto

In the summer of 1930 Rabindranath Tagore visited our university at Marburg and delivered the lecture which is reprinted in this book. We were very deeply impressed by the dignified appearance of this noble Aryan from the East who combined simplicity with dignity, the form of art with spiritual content, and an all-embracing humanism with individual originality. He spoke to us about his faith. We were most impressed by the fact that he did neither dilate upon theories of comparative religion nor did he give us an abridged survey of Indian religion—he simply made us participate in his very personal religious experience, an experience which cannot be separated from this man and his individual life, but which because of its peculiar immediacy and through the impact of self-expression confronted us with the question as to what we know of religious experience and whether we have some substance of our own.

For this reason I want to publish this confession of Tagore in this book. I do not intend to use this confession in support of my own theology, nor do I want to pigeonhole it according to my categories of comparative religion. I feel again the great difference between the spirit of the Upanishads and the spirit that took its rise on the soil of Palestine and spread all over the world; the difference between the religion of the poet and the religion of the biblical prophets to which I owe allegiance. But I as well as others who are conscious of the Christian religion felt even more deeply the enlivening impact of this profound personal experience and the refreshing stimulus which it gave to our own thought.

Tagore emphasizes that he is free from alien sentiments and imitation. Nevertheless he stresses the inheritance of his Vedic ancestors, and the similarity between their and his way of experience and interpreting the world. And, indeed, his roots are deeply embedded in the Indian soil. Some people have tried to interpret Tagore as a poet in the English tradition, they did not know that Tagore, though a modern poet, is part of a specific Bengali school of poets which he himself has rediscovered and interpreted. But even more so, there is indeed the old spirit of the Upanishads in his work.

When I visited Tagore, while he was touring Germany in the course of his previous journey, I asked him personally whether any one of the old holy scriptures of India had been of specific importance to him. He gave the answer which I had expected. He told me that his father had liked the IsaUpanishad best of all, and that he had read it with him, and that he himself had been greatly moved by the spirit of this fine piece of poetry. I therefore want to publish this Upanishad as an appendix to his own confession of faith. It is very interesting to see how the old religious experience arises here again in a modern soul, and it is even more informative to witness how the old heritage takes on a new shape in this present form, and how it expresses itself in a very unique way in the individual form of this highly original man.

CHAPTER 7

Correspondence between Prof. Rudolf Eucken and Rabindranath Tagore

(This correspondence was first published in the Tagore Volume of the Calcutta Municipal Gazette. Tagore himself seems to have thought of these letters as the best summary of his impressions of Germany. The translation of Eucken's letter which was published in the Calcutta Municipal Gazette is so literal that it is almost unintelligible. The text given below is an edited extract of Eucken's letter.)

Prof. Eucken to Tagore

Jena, June 11, 1921

Dear Sir and Master,

I very much regret not having been able to meet you in Germany because I am hard pressed by work But I must send you my greetings and tell you how sorry I am for having missed you. I should like to assure you of my sympathy and my appreciation of your noble work. We are both united by a common aim: we want to raise mankind to a higher level of inner consciousness. This task may be of a different nature in Germany and in India, but our final aim remains the same. There is a profound lesson in our German way of life: the combination of work and soul...In this modern world, however, work and soul have been torn asunder; our culture has become a one-sided culture of labour, and the soul has lost its power to unite the whole of life in harmony. At the same time we have experienced a national and ethical defeat, and we have to worry about the existence of our heavily depressed people. But however dim this aspect of our life may be, we need not despair, because misfortune will not break our courage. In our German way of life there is a great depth and a great capacity for devotion. Even after heavy blows the German nation has always found itself again and has recovered despite pain and sorrow ... In the midst of this danger and distress it is a great pleasure and help to us to hear the voice of the noble Indian philosopher and to be encouraged by him. There will be certainly many things in our present life in Germany which may not please you. The outward appearance often predominates, the surface of our present day life is marked by many scars and rifts, and multifarious movements work at cross purposes. But all this does not affect the depth of German life and I request you not to lose your faith in the German people and their capacity to work ... Germany wants to believe in a new content of life, she does not think along the lines of psychological reactions but looks to metaphysical foundations. In striving for this aim the German and the Indian way of thinking can supplement each other.

Tagore's reply :

Neues Palais, Darmstadt, June 13, 1221

Dear Master,

It has given me great delight to read your kind letter addressed to me. I had a desire to visit Jena and meet you there, but my engagement at Darmstadt has unfortunately upset my plan and it grieves my heart to leave Germany without seeing you. It has been said in our scriptures that there are three ways of realizing the Infinite according to the temperament of individuals. These are through knowledge, through love and through action. Their respective paths are philosophy, religion, and science. But owing to the distraction of selfish psssions and want of detachment men almost everywhere have missed their chance; and philosophy wrongly pursued, religion wrongly practised, and science wrongly applied have brought upon us continual series of disasters. It was the mission of Europe to inaugurate the era of *Karma-yoga,* the fulfilment of self through action. And therefore the vehicle on which she was to travel to her goal, she is made to carry on her head. She has suffered and the world is eagerly waiting to see how she takes the lesson of her sufferings. If it be the destiny of Germany to go through the penance for the sin of the modern age and come out purified and strong, if she can know how to make use of the fire that has scorched her for lighting up a path to the great future, to the aspiration of the soul for its true freedom; she will be blessed in the history of humanity.

I carry with me the most generous hospitality of heart offered to me by the people of this country and I leave behind me my love and sympathy for them.

Yours sincerely

Rabindranath Tagore

CHAPTER 8

The Child
Rabindranath Tagore

In 1930 Tagore attended the famous "Passion Play' at Oberammergau, a village in Bavaria. This play which portrays the suffering of Christ is performed by the villagers once in every ten years in fulfilment of a vow. Tagore was very much impressed by this play, and when he was asked by a German film company for a script dealing with Indian life, he composed this poem in one night in Berlin. It is the only poem which he ever wrote directly in English free verse. The plan of producing a film based on a script by Tagore never materialized, but this poem remains with us as a testimony of a sudden inspiration and a surprising vision.

I

'What of the night?' they ask.
No answer comes.
For the blind Time gropes in a maze and knows not
    its path or purpose.
The darkness in the valley stares like the dead
    eye-sockets of a giant,
  The clouds like a nightmare oppress the sky,
  and the massive shadows lie scattered like the torn
    limbs of the night.

A lurid glow waxes and wanes on the horizon,–
is it an ultimate threat from an alien star,
    or an elemental hunger licking the sky?
Things are deliriously wild,
they are a noise whose grammar is a groan,
    and words smothered out of shape and sense.
They are the refuse, the rejections, the fruitless failures of life, abrupt ruins of prodigal pride,—
fragments of a bridge over the oblivion of a vanished stream, godless shrines that shelter reptiles,
    marble steps that lead to blankness.
Sudden tumults rise in the sky and wrestle
    and a startled shudder runs along the sleepless hours.
Are they from desperate floods
    hammering against their cave walls,
or from some fanatic storms
    whirling and howling incantations?
Are they the cry of an ancient forest
    flinging up its hoarded fire in a last extravagant suicide,
or screams of a paralytic crowd scourged by lunatics blind and deaf?
Underneath 'the noisy terror' a stealthy hum creeps up
    like bubbling volcanic mud,
  a mixture of sinister whispers, rumours and
    slanders, and hisses of derision.
The men gathered there are vague like torn pages of an epic.
Groping in groups or single, their torchlight tattoos their
    faces in chequered lines, in patterns of frightfulness.
The maniacs suddenly strike their neighbours on suspicion
and a hubbub of an indiscriminate fight bursts forth
    echoing from hill to hill.
The women weep and wail,
  they cry that their children are lost in a wilderness
    of contrary paths with confusion at the end.

Others defiantly ribald shake with raucous laughter
their lascivious limbs unshrinkingly loud,
for they think that nothing matters.

II

There on the crest of the hill
stands the Man of faith amid the snow-white silence,
He scans the sky for some signal of light,
and when the clouds thicken and the nightbirds
scream as they fly,
he cries, 'Brothers, despair not, for Man is great'.

But they never heed him.
for they believe that the elemental brute is eternal
and goodness in its depth is darkly cunning in deception.

When beaten and wounded they cry, 'Brother, where art thou?'
The answer comes, 'I am by your side.'—
But they cannot see in the dark
and they argue that the voice is of their own desperate desire,
that men are ever condemned to fight for phantoms
in an interminable desert of mutual menace.

III

The clouds part, the morning star appears in the East,
a breath of relief springs up from the heart of the earth,
the murmur of leaves ripples along the forest path,
and the early bird sings.

'The time has come,' proclaims the Man of faith.
'The time for what?'
'For the pilgrimage.'
They sit and think, they know not the meaning,
and yet they seem to understand according to their desires.

The touch of the dawn goes deep into the soil
and life shivers along through the roots of all things.
'To the pilgrimage of fulfilment: a small voice whispers,
nobody knows whence.

Taken up by the crowd
    it swells into a mighty meaning.

Men raise their heads and look up,
    women lift their arms in reverence,
    children clap their hands and laugh.

The early glow of the sun shines like a golden garland
    on the forehead of the Man of faith,
and they all cry: 'Brother, we salute thee!'

IV

Men begin to gather from all quarters,
    from across the seas, the mountains and pathless wastes,

They come from the valley of the Nile and banks of the Ganges,
    from the snow-sunk uplands of Tibet,
    from the high-walled cities of glittering towers,
    from the dense dark tangle of savage wilderness.

Some walk, some ride on camels, horses and elephants,
    on chariots with banners vying with the clouds of dawn,

The priests of all creeds burn incense, chanting verses as they go.
    The monarchs march at the head of their armies,
    lances flashing in the sun and drums beating loud.

Ragged beggars and courtiers pompously decorated,
    agile young scholars and teachers burdened
    with learned age jostle each other in the crowd.

Women come chatting and laughing,
mothers, maidens and brides,
    with offerings of flowers and fruit,
    sandal paste and scented water.

Mingled with them is the harlot,
    shrill of voice and loud in tint and tinsel.

The gossip is there who secretly poisons the well
    of human sympathy and chuckles.

The maimed and the cripple join the throng
    with the blind and the sick,

the dissolute, the thief and the man who makes a trade of
his God for profit and mimics the saint.
'The fulfilment!'
They dare not talk aloud,
but in their minds they magnify their own greed,
and dream of boundless power,
of unlimited impunity for pilfering and plunder,
and eternity of feast for their unclean gluttonous flesh.

V

The Man of faith moves on along pitiless paths strewn
with flints over scorching sands and steep mountainous tracks.
They follow him, the strong and the weak, the aged and young,
the rulers of realms, the tillers of the soil.
Some grow weary and footsore, some angry and suspicious.
They ask at every dragging step,
'How much further is the end?'
The Man of faith sings in answer
They scowl and shake their fists and yet they cannot resist him;
the pressure of the moving mass and indefinite
hope push them forward.
They shorten their sleep and curtail their rest,
they out-vie each other in their speed,
they are ever afraid lest they may be too late for their chance
while others be more fortunate.
The days pass,
the ever-receding horizon tempts them with renewed
lure of the unseen till they are sick.
Their faces harden, their curses grow louder and louder.

VI

It is night.
The travellers spread their mats on the ground
under the banyan tree.

A gust of wind blows out the lamp
and the darkness deepens like a sleep into a swoon.

Some one from the crowd suddenly stands up
and pointing to the leader with merciless finger breaks out
'False prophet, thou hast deceived us!'

Others take up the cry one by one,
women hiss their hatred and men growl.

At last one bolder than others suddenly deals him a blow.

They cannot see his face, but fall upon him in fury of destruction
and hit him till he lies prone upon the ground his life extinct.

The night is still, the sound of the distant waterfall comes muffled,
and a faint breath of jasmine floats in the air.

VII

The pilgrims are afraid.
The women begin to cry, the men in an agony of wretchedness
shout at them to stop.

Dogs break out barking and are cruelly whipped into
silence broken by moans.

The night seems endless and men and women begin to
wrangle as to who among them was to blame.

They shriek and shout and as they are ready to unsheathe their knives,
the darkness pales, the morning light overflows
the mountain tops.

Suddenly they become still and gasp for breath as they
gaze at the figure lying dead.

The women sob out loud and men hide their faces in their hands.

A few try to slink away unnoticed,
but their crime keeps them chained to their victim.

They ask each other in bewilderment,
'Who will show us the path?'

The old man from the East bends his head and says:
'The Victim.'

They sit still and silent.
Again speaks the old man,
'We refused him in doubt, we killed him in anger,
now we shall accept him in love,
for in his death he lives in the life of us all, the great Victim.'
And they all stand up and mingle their voices and sing,
'Victory to the Victim.'

VIII

'To the pilgrimage' calls the young,
'to love, to power, to knowledge, to wealth overflowing,'
'We shall conquer the world and the world beyond this,'
they all cry exultant in a thundering cataract of voices,
The meaning is not the same to them all, but only the impulse,
the moving confluence of wills that recks not death
and disaster.
No longer they ask for their way,
no more doubts are there to burden their minds
or weariness to clog their feet.
The spirit of the Leader is within them and ever beyond them—
the Leader who has crossed death and all limits.
They travel over the fields where the seeds are sown,
by the granary where the harvest is gathered,
and across the barren soil where famine dwells
and skeletons cry for the return of their flesh.
They pass through populous cities humming with life,
through dumb desolation hugging its ruined past,
and hovels for the unclad and unclean,
a mockery of home for the homeless.
They travel through long hours of the summer day,
and as the light wanes in the evening they ask
the man who reads the sky:
'Brother, is yonder the tower of our final hope and peace?'
The wise man shakes his head and says:

'It is the last vanishing cloud of the sunset.'
'Friends', exhorts the young, 'do not stop.
Through the night's blindness we must struggle
into the Kingdom of the living light.'

They go on in the dark.
The road seems to know its own meaning.
and dust under foot dumbly speaks of direction.

The stars – celestial wayfarers – sing in silent chorus:
'Move on, comrades!'

In the air floats the voice of the Leader:
'The goal is nigh.'

IX

The first flush of dawn glistens on the dew-dripping
leaves of the forest.

The man who reads the sky cries:
'Friends. we have come!'

They stop and look around.
On both sides of the road the corn is ripe to the horizon,
–the glad golden answer of the earth to the morning light.

The current of daily life moves slowly
between the village near the hill and the one by the river bank.

The potter's wheel goes round, the woodcutter brings fuel to the
market,
the cowherd takes his cattle to the pasture,
and the woman with pitcher on her head walks to the well.

But where is the King's castle, the mine of gold,
the secret book of magic,
the sage who knows love's utter wisdom?

'The stars cannot be wrong' assures the reader of the sky.
'Their signal points to that spot.'

And reverently he walks to a wayside spring
from which wells up a stream of water, a liquid light, like the
morning melting into a chorus of tears and laughter.

Near it in a palm grove surrounded by a strange hush stands a leaf-
thatched hut.
at whose portal sits the poet of the unknown shore, and sings:
'Mother, open the gate !'

X

A ray of morning sun strikes aslant at the door.
The assembled crowd feel in their blood the primeval chant of
creation:
'Mother, open the gate?'
The gate opens,
The mother is seated on a straw-bed with the babe on her lap,
Like the dawn with the morning star.
The sun's ray that was waiting at the door outside
falls on the head of the child.
The poet strikes his lute and sings out:
'Victory to Man, the new-born, the ever-living.'
They kneel down – the king and the beggar, the saint and the sinner,
The wise and the fool, – and cry:
'Victory to Man, the new-born, the ever-living.'
The old man from the East murmurs to himself:
'I have seen!'

Biographical Notes

Paul Natorp (1854-1924), professor of philosophy at Marburg University, one of the most important representatives of the so-called Neo-Kantian school of thought. He was also one of the intellectual leaders of the German Youth Movement which arose at the turn of the century in protest against the cant and artificiality of the Victorian era.

Rudolf Otto (1869-1937), professor of theology and religious philosophy at Marburg University, one of the founders of comparative religious studies in Germany. His main work *The Holy* and his essay on "Mysticism in East and West" as well as his studies of the philosophical systems of Ramanuja and his disciples established important categories of the study of world religions.

Count Hermann Keyserling (1880-1946) philosopher and essayist. His Indian Travel Diary of a Philosopher which appeared in 1921 was widely read at that time. He established the "School of Wisdom" at Darmstadt in 1920 at the invitation of the Duke of Hesse-Darmstadt. In 1921 he invited Tagore to lecture at this school. Keyserling wrote against the one-sided rule of the intellect and advocated the cultivation of wisdom which is based on a deeper intuitive understanding of man and nature.

Rudolf Eucken (1846-1926) was professor of philosophy at Jena University. He published several books on philosophy and religion and was awarded the Nobel Prize for Literature in 1908. He strove for a spiritual life based on an understanding of one's self and a universal appreciation of reality.

***Helmuth von Glasenapp** (born* 1891*) professor of Indology at Berlin and Tuebingen Universities. His many books on Indian philosophy and religion have contributed to a better understanding of Indian thought by the general reader. He reviewed many of Tagore's poems and plays in contemporary newspapers.

---

*Glasenapp died in 1963.

Bibliography

P. Cremer, *Rabindranath Tagore*, Vol. XI of "Dichter der Moderne" Berlin, Borngraeber 1914 (first biography of Tagore in a European language)

H. Meyer-Benfey, *Rabindranath Tagore*, Berlin 1921

P. Natorp, *Stunden mit Rabindranath Thakkur*, Jena 1921

E. Engelhardt, *Rabindranath Tagore als Mensch, Dichter und Philosoph*, Furche Verlag 1921

Arthur Schurig, *Tagore, seine Persoenlichkeit, seine Werke, seine Weltanschauung*, Dresden 1921

Hanns Fiedler, *Die Welt im Drama Tagores, Der Dramatiker und der Sinn seines Werkes*, Berl in 1922

Fritz Toegel, *Rabindranath Tagore und seine Sendung*, Leipzig 1922

Friedrich Heiler, *Christlicher Glaube und indisches Geistesleben : Rabindranath Tagore, Mahatma Gandhi, Brahmabandhav Upadhyaya, Sadhu Sundar Singh*, 1926

W. Graefe, *Die Weltanschauung Rabindranath Tagores und ihre Beziehung zum Abendland* (Dissertation) 1930

Rudolf Otto, *Rabindranath Tagores Bekenntnis*, Marburg 1931

M. Winternitz, *Rabindranath Tagore : Religion und Weltanschauung des Dichters*. Prag 1936

Articles in periodical publications:

M. Groener, Rabindranath Tagore, Archiv fuer systematische Philosophie N. F. Vol. XXII, 351-367 (1917)

M. Kaubisch, Rabindranath Tagore, Preussische Jahrbuecher, Berlin, Vol. CLXXXII, 18/-194 (1920)

J. Overmans, Indische Gedanken ueber die Kultur des Abendlandes, Stimmen der Zeit, Vol. C, 172-177 (1920)

M. Meyer-Benfey, Rabindranath Tagore, Christllche Welt, Vol. XXXIV (1920)

TAGORE AND GERMANY

Satinder Kumar Lambah

This is the English translation of an article which appeared in the Journal "Indien in der Gegenwart" published by ICCR in 1996 when the author was Ambassador of India in Germany

Tagore and Germany

Satinder Kumar Lambah

The foundation of relations between Germany and India lay in the intellectual and cultural exchanges, started more than three centuries ago. Early German scholars contributed immensely to the discovery and the serious study of ancient Indian philosophy, literature and languages in the West. By the later half of the nineteenth century, Indian philosophers and writers had begun to travel to the West, contributing to the organic growth of this intellectual dialogue.

Rabindranath Tagore ranks as one of the greatest voices of modern India. In a life of eighty years from 1861 to 1941, which almost parallels the saga of awakening and struggle for freedom in India, Tagore distinguished himself as one of the greatest writers and poets in the world. A gifted music composer, he introduced a new school of music, now named after him; championed the revival of traditional dance forms; gave shape to his unique vision of education by establishing the world known Viswa Bharati; and turned in later years into a painter, as well. He provided a moral and spiritual impulse to India's struggle for Independence. His works reflected the soul of India, not merely in its philosophical underpinnings, but also in the throbbing of everyday life.

It was inevitable, as India sought to find her place under the sun, that Rabindranath Tagore should become a spiritual ambassador of

India to the world, interpreting through his works and lectures, the timeless message of an ancient country to a world that, in the wake of the First World War, was restless, confused and uncertain. Tagore himself was keenly interested in the world outside, in the progress and achievements of different societies and in relations among peoples. At an address given at Milan in 1921, he confessed to a "*a great desire to make my pilgrimage to the shrine of humanity, where the human mind was fully awake, with all its lamp lighted, there* to *meet face to face the Eternal in Man*". Moved by this impulse, Tagore travelled extensively especially in the 1910 and 1920, visiting several countries in Asia, Europe and America. He was received everywhere with extraordinary enthusiasm and support.

During these visits, he articulated his vision of the world (perhaps best summarized in that moving poem, "Where the mind is without fear ..... .") as one which has *"not been broken into fragments by narrow domestic walls"*. His vision was cast in a spiritual and humanistic light, in seeking to *"study the mind of man* in *its realization of different aspects of truth from diverse points of view"*. Perhaps, it was also based in the constraints that the German readers faced in fully appreciating Tagore.

Though after the war the first book of poems translated directly from Bengali appeared, it did not set a trend of similar efforts. Germans continued to read Tagore mainly through translations of the English versions. Most of his translations focused on the romantic aspects and lyricism in his poetry. The entire gamut of his poetic expressions – philosophical, existential, realist, in addition to romantic – did not, therefore, reach a large section of the readers. It was, perhaps, the publication in 1982 of the first direct translation from Bengali by Gisela Leiste of the voluminous novel "Gora" that has set off efforts for more direct translation from Bengali into German of Tagore's works. Alokeranjan Dasgupta, from South Asian Institute of Heidelberg University, published in 1987 "The Other Tagore", a collection of Tagore poems in German. He has, of course, provided an important bridge between Bengali and German literature. He has translated several German authors, including Heine, Brecht, Kroetz, etc. into Bengali. The significance of "The Other Tagore" lies in it being regarded as a first serious attempt to produce a poetically adequate translation of Tagore poetry from Bengali to German and in exposing the German readers to the existential and philosophical poems of Tagore. Dr. Martin Kämpchen, who has Ph.D degrees in German Literature from Vienna and a Comparative Religion from Visva Bharati, has been living in India since 1973. He has translated directly from Bengali into German two volumes of poetry by Tagore and has also written his biography in German.

Tagore must count as an important literary phenomenon of the twentieth century Germany. He was one of the most important bridges of dialogue between India and Germany in the long history of cultural and intellectual exchange between the two countries. He was an outstanding messenger of the wisdom and the rich heritage of ancient Indian philosophy. But, his vision of humanity was Universal, in which the artificial divisions between man and man dissolved. Above all, he was one of the greatest creative talents of the century.

Perhaps, one of the most moving tributes came to him on his seventieth birthday from Albert Einstein, who wrote, *"you saw Creation engulfed in wild battles from want and dark desires. You saw salvation in silent contemplation and in the works of beauty. Cultivating the same you dedicated your long and fruitful life to the service of mankind, spreading universally the sense of benevolence and open-mindedness heralded by the wise men of your people".*

Tagore himself appeared to have gained immensely from his contacts with people throughout the world or, what he would describe in his inimitable style, as *"invitation to this world's festival".* He wrote that *"the whole world with its ideas have come close to me... Today, I am on the point of unifying my country and its thoughts with that of other countries in the world".* Emphasizing the vitality of cultural interaction, he warned the inward looking nationalists in India that *"our present struggle to alienate our heart and mind from the West is a spiritual suicide"*. Tagore's mission of creating a bridge of understanding between the "East" and the "West" appears to have been personally rewarding, as well.

It was due to the profound but simple and lyrical poetry, and the humanism and spirituality in Tagore's creative expression, that people in Germany, amidst the chaos of a military upheaval, political uncertainty and economic hardships, welcomed him in multitudes. Tagore came to Germany three times – in 1921, 1926 and 1930.

Extensive material exists on Tagore's visits to several countries, but comprehensive research and documentation on his relationship with Germany is not available, even though by "all accounts his popularity in Germany in the 1920s was unparalleled. Alex Aronson's *Rabindranath through Western Eyes,* which appeared in 1943, *Tagore in Germany* edited by Dietmar Rothermund and, more recently, Martin Kämpchen's *Rabindranath Tagore and Germany* are among the most valuable studies on the subject.

By the time Tagore made his first trip to Germany in 1921, the Nobel Prize had brought into the consciousness of the Western audience this unknown man from Bengal; the translations of his books were available in several European languages and he was already a known figure in Germany. The first German edition of "Gitanjali" had been published by the famous Kurt Wolff Verlag in 1914. During his visit in 1921, Count Graf Hermann Keyserling hosted a "Tagore Week" in Darmstadt, in which the writer-philosopher himself participated. Tagore also visited Hamburg, Mannheim and Berlin. Tagore's lecture in Berlin on 2nd June drew such a tremendous response that it could only begin half an hour late, after it was announced that the lecture would be repeated the next day. His enormous popularity in Germany translated into sales of one million copies of his books by 1923.

Tagore's second trip to Germany in 1926 took him to thirteen cities, from Hamburg to Munich, from Dresden to Stuttgart. During his five day stay in Berlin from 11-15 September, he spoke at the Philharmonie. Receptions were held in his honour by Culture

Minister Carl Heinrich Becker and by the Reichspräsident von Hindenburg, who also accepted Tagore's proposal for exchange of guest professors with Visva Bharati in Santiniketan.

The last visit to Germany came in 1930 at age of sixty-nine, two years after Tagore had taken to painting and sketching. He brought 300 of his artistic works to Germany. Exhibitions of his works opened simultaneously in Berlin, Munich and Dresden.

The reaction to Tagore's visits to Germany, especially in 1921, was not unanimous across the entire spectrum of his audience. The public at large received him with unbridled adulation, seen in the near frenzied ovation he received wherever he went. A "Tagore Mania" appears to have developed in Germany in 1921. But, the focus – and the apparent cause for the response – was more to do with the Tagore the person than Tagore the writer. The image of a saint, mystic, healer, "a Light from the East", was fuelled by his roots in an exotic, remote land and by his appearance, clothing and demeanour, which the public and the Press tended to concentrate on.

The Press gave extensive coverage to his visit, and, as was to be expected, devoted a good part of their attention to his persona. Eight years earlier in 1913, the conferment of the Nobel Prize on Tagore was received in Germany without any enthusiasm to say the least. The disappointment and dismay stemmed in part from the lack of awareness about Tagore, but apparently also from the belied expectations of the award going to the Austrian writer Peter Rosegger. In 1921, Tagore was no stranger. While one section of the Press was ecstatic and adoring, another group was resentful, not so much about his works, on which they were generally appreciative, but about the image of Tagore which had been built up. Some of them, it has been argued, reacted from cultural and spiritual envy. A newspaper wrote, not entirely without merit, that there were writers in Germany who too deserved to be celebrated and made famous in foreign countries. Another argued that Tagore's message was nothing but the elementary and basic Christian world-view. The differences in perceptions and opinions are natural, but the reactions serve to highlight the extraordinary interest in Tagore in Germany of the 1920s.

Of great interest to anyone studying Tagore's relationship with Germany is the attitude of the contemporary German writers and scholars. It is well known that German writers did not, by and large, share the public enthusiasm for Tagore. Some like Rainer Maria Rilke, Thomas Mann, Stefan Zweig and Hermann Hesse wrote about Tagore or had dialogue with him. There were several, including Gerhart Hauptmann and Heinrich Mann, whose works have no reference to Tagore. Among those who did write on Tagore, the opinions varied from negative to indifference to generous appreciation.

The guarded response of the writers, in contrast to the public response, has been the subject of many conjectures, astonishment, perhaps dismay, at the popular fanfare surrounding Rabindranath Tagore, the aura of the exotic surrounding him, the overemphasis on the "mystic" or "missionary of the Spirit" aspects rather than on the poet and writer, and, the fact that Tagore's works in German were translated from the English translation of the original Bengali writings.

Thomas Mann wrote: *"I am familiar with isolated, intensely soulful poems of his which, however, reading them in Gennan, made no immediate impression on me,* as *indeed is the case with all translated poetry".* While Stefan Zweig was moved to exclaim, *"Such serenity, supreme beauty",* and Bertolt Brecht was equally generous in his appreciation, Hermann Hesse, whose ancestors had lived in India and who himself was very interested in the country, reacted indifferently, if not negatively to "The Gardener", and somewhat positively to the "The Home and the World". Many writers judged Tagore's writings not on merit, but in terms of stereotypes of the "East-West" dichotomy.

There were many German scholars who had with varying levels of involvement interacted with or wrote on Tagore. Some like Keyserling and Rudolf Euken had met Tagore before he received the Nobel Prize; some like Moriz Winternitz, the renowned Indologist from the German University of Prague, and Stella Kramrisch visited Santiniketan and taught there. Several others spent many years with Tagore at Santiniketan. The scholars were generally positive in their appraisal of Tagore, and at any rate focused mainly on his works and his philogophy. Moriz Winternitz described him as one of the greatest world-poets, in whose works the pure human element appealed so strongly that despite the foreign context, one could easily identify with the experience.

How did Tagore react to Germany and the response to his visits? Tagore had great respect and affection for Germany and its intellectual tradition. He once wrote: *"Germany has done more than any country in the world for opening up and broadening the channel of the intellectual and spiritual communication of the West with India".* In a letter written from Hamburg on May 20, 1921 to Count Keyserling on the structure of "Tagore Week" at Darmstadt, he expressed a great desire to interact freely with as many people as possible.

Tagore's strong sense of optimism, faith in the human spirit and his spiritual view of things comes through strongly in his views on Germany in the aftermath of the First World War, written in a letter to Rudolf Euken: *"If it be the destiny of Germany to go through the penance for the sin of the modern age and come out purified and strong, if she can know how to make use of the fire that has scorched her for lighting up the path to a great future, to the aspiration of the soul for its true freedom, she will be blessed in the history of humanity".* He himself remained unaffected, perhaps overwhelmed, by all the adulation that he received in Germany. He expressed his feelings in a letter to C.F. Andrews: *"It has been* a *wonderful experience* in *this country for me! Such fame* as *I have got I cannot take seriously. It is too readily given; and too immediately. It has not had the perspective of time. And this* is *why I feel frightened and tired at it and even sad."* The sixtieth birthday greetings from German authors, accompanied by a gift of four hundred copies of German books, had deeply touched him and he felt certain that *"it will find response in the hearts of my countrymen."*

While Tagore had become a household name in Germany in the 1920s, he did not arouse as much interest in the second Post-War era, when once again Germany was gripped by the psychological and social ravages of the war. Perhaps, it was what Hesse described in 1957 as a *"phenomenon based on a universal historical truth. Today's man of fame falls into oblivion after his death, and only after a lapse of time ..... sometimes prolonged ..... does the world take the trouble to re-examine ... "*.

Tagore found a home in the hearts of millions of Germans through several decades, giving them, as he has to readers in India and elsewhere, boundless joy and a glimpse of rare beauty and higher order of things. That Tagore continues to hold enormous interest in Germany became evident in the several events held in 1996 in Germany to mark the seventy-fifth anniversary to his first visit to Germany (1921). On the Tagore Day organized by the Indian Institute in Munich on 26th January, 1996 at the Handelskammer, over 250 people packed the hall with a capacity of 150 to hear renowned actor Jochen Striebeck read selections from Dr. Martin Kämpchen's *"that will translate into Unity of Man"*. Ascribing the destruction of peace in part to the dominance of the nation over the individual, he nevertheless expressed great faith in humanity, which *"like the sun can be clouded, but never extinguished."*

At the Indian Cultural Centre in Berlin, the well attended Tagore Anniversary, held on 10th May, 1996, featured a lecture on "Tagore and Germany" by Dr. Joachim Oesterheld of Humböldt University, reading from German translations of Tagore's works and songs by Indian and German students of Rabindra Sangeet. The "Initiative für Frieden und Interculturelle Multiethnische Verbindungen e.v." held a Tagore Symposium on the theme of "Plurality of the Plural World - Conflict and Unity" in August 1996, quite appropriately at the House of World Cultures in Berlin, to celebrate the seventy-fifth anniversary of Tagore's first visit to Germany.

The time is appropriate to once again renew our efforts to make Tagore's works more widely available to German readers and to assessing the impact Tagore made on the world literature in this century, his contribution in advancing human thought and his extraordinary contribution in bringing the people of Germany and India closer.

RABINDRANATH TAGORE AND GERMANY

THREE ESSAYS

A Tribute on the Poet's 150th Birth Anniversary

Martin Kämpchen

These three essays are based on lectures I have delivered in India and Bangladesh. I have eliminated overlapping material as much as feasible, except when I needed to preserve the cohesion of the text.

PREFACE

This section contains three essays on Rabindranath Tagore written over the last few years. They have been delivered as lectures and published in journals previously; here they are brought together in book-form for the first time. I have admitted some overlapping information, rather than destroying the context of each essay. In the back please find my bio-data and a list of my books on Tagore. In the text I refer to my own books using the bracketed numbers given in my booklist. The photos on Tagore reproduced here are from the Rabindra-Bhavan, Visva-Bharati, Santiniketan. I thank the director for the permission to use them.

For twenty years now I have worked on Rabindranath Tagore. During this time, my German translations of Rabindranath's poetry, my German biography and several studies on Tagore's relationship with Germany have appeared. Tagore has been made known to a wider public, he has been established as a figure of world literature. These essays inform and reflect on the role the Indian poet has played in the German history of the 20th century and present a vision for the future.

I thank Mr. Anand Singh Bawa for making it possible for me to publish these essays in the present volume in celebration of the Poet's 150th birthday anniversary in 2011.

CHAPTER 1

Rabindranath Tagore
From "Mystic" to Figure in World Literature

It was in the middle of the year 1976. I was teaching my last German class at the Ramakrishna Mission Institute of Culture. For three years I had been a teacher of mostly college boys and girls; many of them had continued learning from me for three years, others for two years. A good number of former students had joined to give me a friendly farewell. They made me various presents; one of them was a book in Bengali. At the time I could not read Bengali. I was about to leave West Bengal and settle in Madras. I was not sure whether I would return to Kolkata, except for brief visits. When I asked what book they were presenting to me, the answer was,

"Rabindranath's *Gitanjali*!"

For some reason I felt very moved. I held up the book and, on the spur of the moment, said to the class,

"I promise, one day I will read this book!"

I kept that promise.

When I decided to return to West Bengal at the end of 1979, I moved to Santiniketan where I am still based. I had not settled in Santiniketan because I felt drawn to Rabindranath. True, I had read the English *Gitanjali* and some other slim books and was charmed by them. But I had no foreboding that Rabindranath would soon occupy such a central position in my life. When I began studying Bengali in all sincerity, I also struggled through a few simple poems by Rabindranath, mostly from *Gitanjali* to practise my Bengali. Solely for my own benefit, I made a rough translation of several poems. When I compared the Bengali originals with the English renderings by the Poet himself, I was both flabbergasted and aghast.

The English renderings were lovely, full of tender emotions, full of devotional and mildly erotic allusions. Bengali readers who have been nurtured on classical Vaishnava poetry, may not find the imagery of Rabindranath all that striking. But for European readers these images, mystical and sensual at the same time, were – and still are – unusual and original. The constant play on the identity of love of God and love of Woman, the intimacy between God/Woman and man, the yearning to go forever beyond onto a transcendental plane, and yet the earthy love of nature and of cosmic reality – these polarities and contradictions are given a fascinating poetic shape.

Yet, as Aurobindo Ghose, the *Rishi* of Pondicherry, said, "One has only to compare this English prose, beautiful as it is, with the original poetry to see how much has gone out with the change; something is successfully substituted which may satisfy the English reader, but can never satisfy the ear or the mind that once listened to the singer's own native and magical melodies."[1]

Comparing the two versions of the same poem – the Bengali original, and the English text in lyrical prose – both written by the Poet, has taught me the power of verse and rhyme. Both versions express the same thoughts and the same imagery – yet see the enormous difference which versification and rhyme make in the mood, the melody – the sheer magic of a text! In his letters to William Rothenstein, Rabindranath later revealed his anxiety about having achieved the Nobel Prize, and with it world fame, with poetic products which were quite inferior to his original Bengali poetry.

[1]Aurobindo Ghosh, "On Tagore." In: *Golden Book of Tagore*, Calcutta 1931, p.91.

After the Nobel Prize, the English version of *Gitanjali* was swiftly translated into other European languages including German. In Germany, the highly acclaimed Kurt Wolff Verlag, which among others published Franz Kafka, brought out the German *Gitanjali* in 1914. The British publisher Macmillan had offered the book for translation when the Nobel Prize had not yet been declared. One of Kurt Wolff's assistants read the book and, rejecting it, he delivered it to the Post Office to be sent back to London. On that very day, the Nobel Prize winner of 1913 was declared on the radio. Kurt Wolff rushed to the General Post Office of Leipzig and retrieved the packet from a big heap of postal articles. Later, Kurt Wolff never admitted that the book had been rejected first. Instead, he who was still in the beginning of a meteoric career, prided himself of publishing a Nobel Laureate who was to become his first best-selling author. His records show that, all Tagore books combined, Kurt Wolff sold over a million copies.

The beginning of Tagore translation

I shall not write about the rise of Rabindranath's fame in Germany in the 1920s, his special interest in Germany, his contacts with German writers and scholars, and Germany's fascination for Tagore. I have dealt with these subjects in several books[2]. Therefore I focus on my involvement with Tagore studies and Tagore translation.

Noticing the contrast between the Bengali and the English versions of Tagore's poetry, I realised that outside West Bengal and Bangladesh the discovery of Rabindranath, the poet, was yet to come. This led me to the decision, in a bout of youthful, carefree audacity, to work on a volume of German translation from the original Bengali. These German translations were meant to be poetically solid, literarily valid poems in their own right. I discovered that, strangely, the stream of English translations of Rabindranath's poems that had appeared until then, did not consist of serious English poems at all. They were careful reproductions of a surface meaning, mostly without any concern for verse, rhythm, sentence melody or rhyme.

[2]See the book-list at the end of chapter 3.

It so happened that around the time I had taken that decision, Herder Publishers in Germany with whom I already had several books in print, suggested to bring out an anthology of Tagore poetry in German language. The publisher's idea had been that I select my collection from the existing English translations. I rejected this idea, telling them that the time had come to turn back to the source of Rabindranath's poetic genius, to his Bengali poetry. And I advocated a selection translated from Bengali. But I did not feel ready to undertake this colossal assignment. Where to begin? How to select? It was not possible to read even the more important poems one by one. Besides, my Bengali was too limited to appreciate the complex hymnic and narrative poems; they need a background in Sanskrit to comprehend. I had to stick to poetry within my range.

There are two persons who had in the past tried their hand on translating Rabindranath from Bengali to German, although on a limited scale. They were Helene Meyer-Franck and Alokeranjan Dasgupta. Meyer-Franck had been the principal translator of Rabindranth's English prose in the 1920s. Later, over a span of several years, she learnt Bengali, solely assisted by a Bengali student, and solely in order to translate Rabindranath's poetry. At the end of her life, she brought out a lovely, slender book.[3] Although her efforts are unique and daring, I am not quite convinced of the quality of her translations. Going back to the originals, I found many translations to be philologically inexact and too free. Alokeranjan Dasgupta and Lothar Lutze have jointly printed a book entitled *Der andere Tagore* (The other Tagore)[4] which focussed on the later poems. In the book, I felt a marked opposition to the lyrical and devotional side of Rabindranath. I can see how many intellectuals react to it adversely, preferring the existential, matter-of-fact, and despairing poet. But I wanted to appreciate the softness *and* the harshness of

[3]Rabindranath Tagore, *Mit meinen Liedern hab ich dich gesucht.* Poems. Translated by Helene Meyer-Franck. Deutscher Literatur-Verlag Otto Melchert, 1946, 79pp.

[4]Rabindranath Thakur, *Der andere Tagore.* Edited by Alokeranjan Dasgupta. Verlag Wolf Mersch, Freiburg 1987, 127pp.

Rabindranath's lyrical output and definitely aimed at a cross-section of his poems from his early phase until his last days.

I hoped that Aloke-da would help me to make a selection and supervise my translation. I had met him once, and I summoned courage and wrote him with my request. The reply on an Indian postcard, scribbled in a fine, tiny hand, was terse. He wrote that he was not going to help me, unless the translation was entirely in his hands.

Around the same time, William Radice had published his own translation of Tagore poetry, his *Selected Poems of Rabindranath Tagore*[5]. Suddenly, I had with these translations, hit upon a model of what I myself had envisioned. I was delighted to see that Radice used annotations in the back of the book for the more careful reader to understand the context of the original poems and the problems involved translating them. Since then, I have seen in William Radice a kind of mentor in the realm of Tagore study. We became friends, and we meet often in India or in Europe. We have worked together on various projects.

William Radice is a recognized poet in England, hence his translations have the shape and the power of an English poem. Ketaki Kushari Dyson, she too a remarkable poet in Bengali and a translator of Rabindranth's poems into English[6], once said that nobody who is not a poet is able to translate Rabindranath's poems competently. This she proclaimed in a seminar at Max Mueller Bhavan Kolkata, with several of us sitting on the panel. It was my turn to speak after her. I kept quiet. Again requested to make my contribution, I said,

"As I am not a poet, I am not authorized to speak."

Ketaki-di, feeling slightly embarrassed, turned to me and asked,

"Have you never written poetry, Martin?"

---

[5]Penguin Books, 1985 with many subsequent editions, also with Penguin India, Delhi.

[6]Rabindranath Tagore, *I Won't Let You Go*. Selected Poems. Translated from Bengali by Ketaki Kushari Dyson. Bloodaxe Books, Newcastle 1991.

"I have", I admitted, "when I was a student. But only one or two of my poems got published."

"You see!" Ketaki-di butted in, relieved. "So you *are* a poet, although a failed poet!"

Even though I was a "(failed) poet", it took a long time to identify my own poetic style as a translator of Rabindranath. I struggled and struggled trying to single out the kind of language in which I wanted to mould Rabindranath's moods and thoughts. Certainly, it should not be the language of German experimental poetry, nor the stately, laid-back poetry of our classical poet, Johann Wolfgang Goethe, or the laconic, prosaic style of Bertolt Brecht. I chose the language of the modern classical poet I most identify with: Rainer Maria Rilke. He is emotional and refined, he is crystal clear in his poetic expression and uses striking images and symbols. He was a seeker of transcendence, a deep, thoughtful, although somewhat morose, human being. All this, I think, goes well with Rabindranath. I read and re-read Rilke's poems, filling my mind with their melody, and only then set off translating Rabindranath's poems.

I started with simple ones, some *Gitanjali*-poems. Simple? – Of course they are not simple by any description. All that makes them a good starting point for a translator is that they have a limited and non-Sanskritic vocabulary, and are short and precise. Rabindranath used rhyme almost throughout his life with the exception of many of his late poems. Rhyme comes easy in Bengali as there are only few endings. Proper and non-artificial rhymes are excruciatingly difficult to set in English. In German, rhyming comes more natural, but it still is not undemanding to translate in rhyme. So when choosing a poem for translation, I first decided whether or not to use rhyme. Some poems just would not get their message across without rhyme. They would be empty, without magic. This is true for many, not all, *Gitanjali* poems, and especially true for the children's poems from *Sisu*.

Rabindranath Tagore, 1913

Santiniketan Ashram landmark—Singha-Sadan

Tagore and his German publisher Kurt Wolff in Germany, 1921

Rabindranath Tagore and the German philosopher Hermann Keyserling (second on the right) in Darmstadt, 1921

Rabindranath Tagore in Germany, 1926

Rabindranath Tagore and Sigmund Freud in Vienna, 1926

Tagore with members of the Youth Movement, Germany 1930

Tagore with Albert Einstein in Berlin, 1930

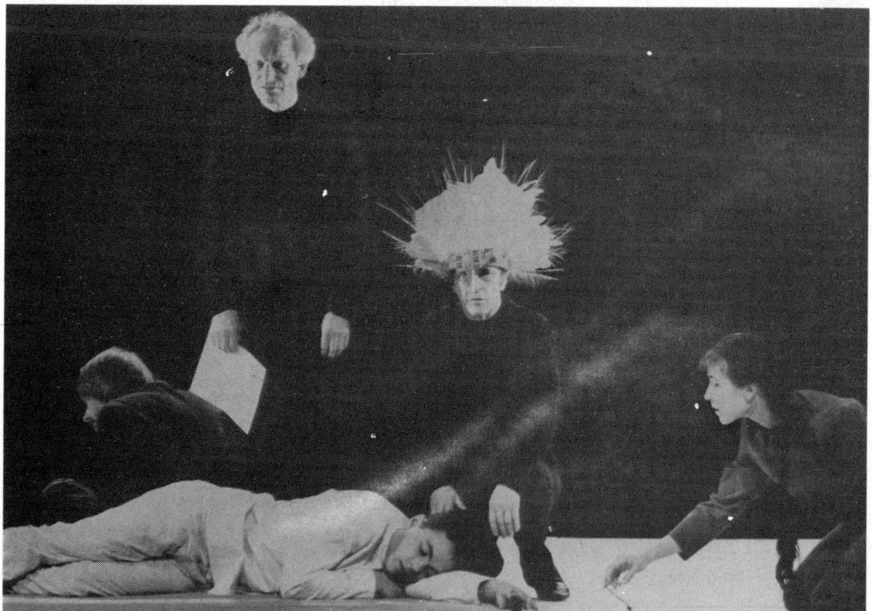

A production of Tagore's play "The Post Office", staged by German theatre director Wolfram Mehring who used Martin Kämpchen's translation

The famous German Buddhist monk Anagarika Govinda (later Lama Govinda) lived with Tagore in Santiniketan

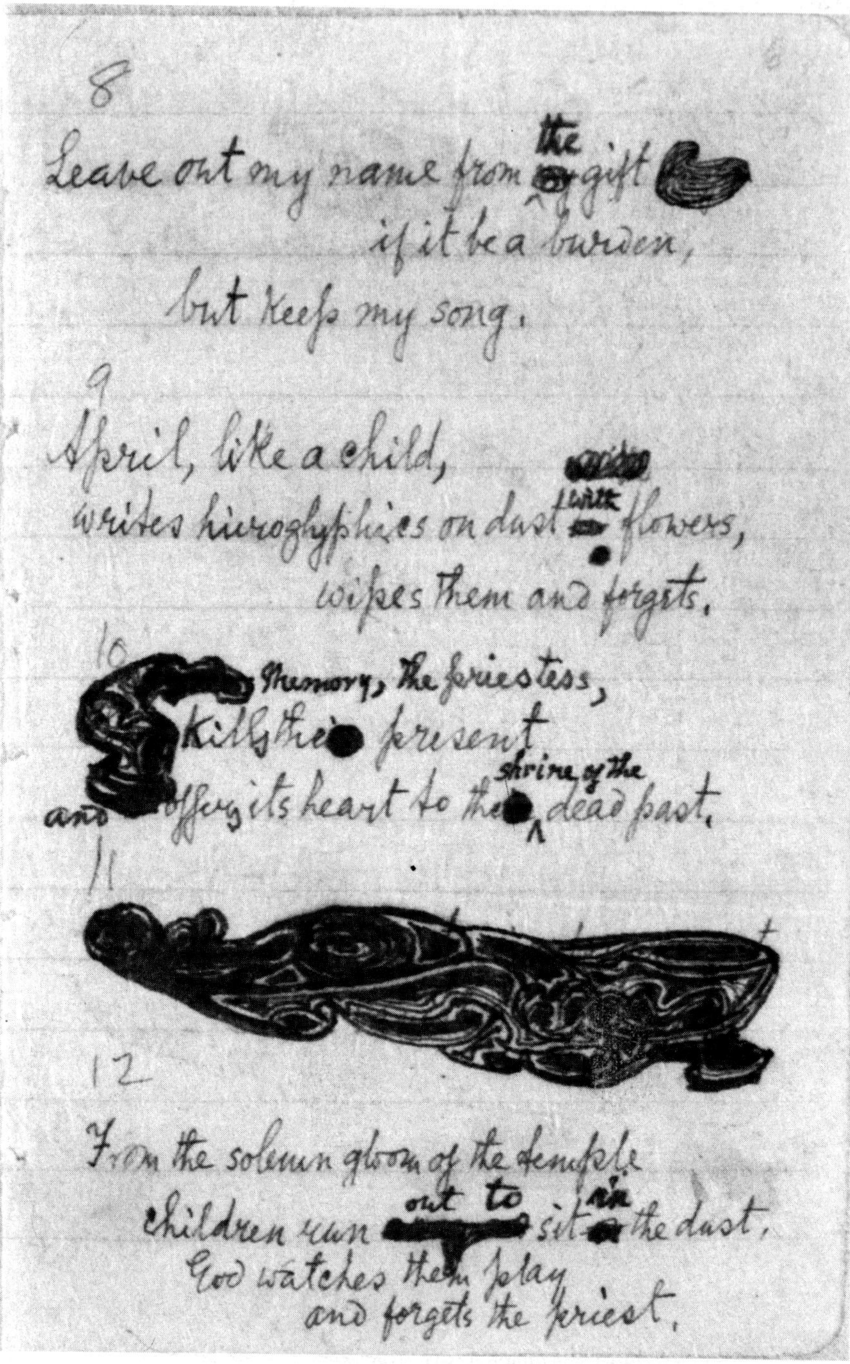

8

Leave out my name from the gift
if it be a burden,
but keep my song.

9

April, like a child,
writes hieroglyphics on dust with flowers,
wipes them and forgets.

10

Memory, the priestess,
kills the present
and offers its heart to the shrine of the dead past.

11

12

From the solemn gloom of the temple
children run out to sit in the dust,
God watches them play
and forgets the priest.

A page from Tagore's manuscript 'Fireflies'

It has often happened that I have chosen a poem for translation and then gave it up in the process. There are two possible reasons. First, the poem proved to be too difficult either transcending the limits of my understanding of Bengali, or too complex to render into a European language. Secondly, while translating I realized that the poetic content of the text was too weak. It surprised me to see that the quality of a poem is revealed in the process of translation. If, however, the poetic content was strong and lucid, and the vocabulary with all its associations and references well within my grasp, then it meant sheer ecstasy to translate the Poet.

Communing with the poem, I become truly a poet myself, not a mere "failed" one. I have noticed that, faced with the Bengali poetic material, my creative energies come to light; suddenly I know which words to choose, my pen assumes an authority which is derived from an unknown source. It is pure delight to have the Poet next to me at such moments. Often I have thought – and express this here, no matter whether some Bengali readers may object – that my *translating* Rabindranath means knowing him more intimately than Bengalis just *reading* him.

Living in Santiniketan gives me the privilege of having many associates who help me with my translation work. When I make a first draft, I like to listen to the poem a number of times in order to internalise its rhythm and melody, its mood. Early on, it was Subarna Roy Chowdhury (now Chatterjee) who did this for me; after her marriage it is now Rajen Sarkar. They look up known and unknown vocabulary. Indeed, I insist on looking up even familiar words in order to have a command over all the layers and shades of its meaning. Any explanation by them has to be in Bengali. This done, I withdraw and work out the German translation alone; this may take many hours and it requires the most intense concentration. I let this second draft rest for a day or longer and then go over it, correcting, reading out the translation to hear whether it "works". Further corrections are effected whenever I re-read the text. Often I have met professors from Visva-Bharati to get help with the interpretation of certain lines.

A translation is never really finished because it has to satisfy the original as well as itself which results in sometimes irreconcilable contradictions. To resolve some of them, I follow William Radice's model and add comprehensive notes to each poem I translate. Whenever I leave out or add a word for the sake of an effective translation, I give a note. If a word has more layers of meaning and association in the original than the word I translate it with can convey, I explain it in a note. Further, cultural contexts are being elucidated as well as the place the poem commands within Rabindranath's literary opus. While I am careful not to overburden my readers, I still hope that in this way the translation receives more "body", more ambivalence, a greater associative wealth.

Tagore translation is weighed down by two vices which I have been fighting. I strongly believe that poetry translation can be done only *into* one's mother tongue, not away from it. A language's fine innuendoes and subtle associations can be intuitively comprehended only by a person who is born in it. Further, poetry cannot be translated by two people, but only by the sensibilities of one individual. Both these rules have been sinned against in Germany as often as in India.

During the years I was busy with working on my anthology of Tagore poems, I received yet another request. I had read and enjoyed the poetic aphorisms by Rabindranath, collected in *Sphulinga*, *Lekhan* and *Konika.* I made a selection of one hundred from these three books and translated them. These crisp sayings with a clear and simple poetic message were easy prey for me and an excellent training ground for more complex poetry. So I dealt with them first. This collection was the first to come out in German [8]*, embellished by photographs by a friend, Andreas Hoffmann. A year thereafter, my selection of fifty poems appeared as a paperback [9]. 7,000 copies were sold, and many poems were reproduced in anthologies and in magazines. A third volume, collecting partly new and partly old translations, was done by Benziger Verlag (Switzerland) [10]. This book contains sensitive black-and-white pictures by another photographer friend, Samiran Nandy of Santiniketan, most of them taken in the rural

*See the book-list at the end of chapter 3.

vicinity of Santiniketan. The majority taken from *Gitanjali* and *Sisu*, these poems could make themselves at home in their original physical and emotional environment.

All three books were published by large, respected Catholic publishers. They had shown an interest in Rabindranath Tagore because he still feeds on the reputation of being a "mystic" and "sage". He is recognised as a religious figure, rather than a writer of repute. Having seen the weak translations into German (done from the Poet's English renderings), in fact many distinguished writers had shown scant interest in him. It was my desire to turn this around with my translations and demonstrate Tagore's true worth as a poet. I reached this aim when Insel Publishers in Frankfurt agreed to print a selection of Tagore's Love Poems [11]. Insel is among a handful of top literary publishers in Germany. On their list of authors are Rilke, Beckett, Hesse and a host of other beloved classical and modern names in world literature. The culmination of this development came in 2005 when another literary publisher, Verlag Artemis und Winkler (Düsseldorf), brought out a *Selected Works of Rabindranath Tagore* in its well-established series "Winkler Weltliteratur" (Winkler World Literature) [12].

The Poet had, finally, arrived in Germany! At long last he is regarded as a figure of world literature on a par with Shakespeare, Tolstoy and Dante. This book reproduced all my published poetry translations and a few new ones, as well as the poems which appeared in *Der andere Tagore*. Further, two short stories and *Caturanga*, translated by Hans Harder, Bengali essays, selected and translated by Rahul Peter Das, two plays, *Dakghar* and *Tasher Desh*, translated by myself, a bunch of letters, selected and translated by Alokeranjan Das Gupta, *Sadhana* translated from the English by Axel Monte and the *Conversations with Albert Einstein*, translated and edited by Andor Orand Carius, all appeared in this volume.

Research on Tagore's visits to Germany

My efforts centering around Rabindranath Tagore had, from the beginning, a two-pronged target: translation as well as research on

Rabindranath's relationship with Germany. Soon after I had decided to translate Rabindranath's poems, I became aware that the story of his three visits to Germany had not yet been told. The biographies had dipped into the English-language sources preserved in the archive of Rabindra-Bhavan, Santiniketan. But, ignoring one flimsy effort, no German-knowing person had recently conducted research on the German material which was buried in Rabindra-Bhavan as well as in archives in Germany. I saw a virgin field of research in front of me. Never having conducted historical research – my two theses had been endeavours at interpretation – I was excited to start something new. Moreover, the year 1991, the 50th death anniversary of Tagore, was drawing close, and the Max Mueller Bhavan planned a series of events to mark it. I suggested a documentation on Tagore's relationship with German writers and scholars. The director granted my request.

This was an opportunity as well as a temptation. I went to the Rabindra-Bhavan day after day to read the content of a few dozen files, making ample notes and copying out page after page by hand. I worked at a feverish pace because there was little time. The book was to be launched in 1991 as the opening of the Tagore Programmes. I went to Germany to continue the research in the Deutsche Literaturarchiv (German Literature Archive) at Marbach (near Stuttgart) which is the central research institute for German Literature. I dug up wonderful material, including letters, newspaper articles, photographs, drawings, and cartoons. Again, a new world opened up for me: I witnessed the "clash" and the mingling of an Indian mind with German society in so many facets. I had studied the era between the two world wars for my first thesis on German Literature. Yet, when I ploughed through these files, it seemed I had not known it at all. The era sprung to life through the frictions and blossoms of the Tagore – Germany interface. *Rabindranath Tagore and Germany: A Documentation* [1] did appear in time, but it contains many loopholes and inadequacies for which I feel sorry now. There had been too little time. Nonetheless, the book impressed Bengali literary society sufficiently to award me the "Rabindra

Puraskar" of the West Bengal government in 1992. The book proved that Rabindranath entertained contacts with many writers and scholars of consequence in the 1920s.

My research continued for about a decade. I visited the Indian Institute of Advanced Study in Shimla as a Fellow in 1995 and 1996 to work on my second book, *Rabindranath Tagore in Germany: Four Responses to a Cultural Icon* [6], which is more mature and complete; however, it deals with only a segment of Rabindranath's involvement with German cultural figures. Meanwhile, in my "Tagore trunk" at Santiniketan, there is material for at least one more book.

Personalities associated with my research

While at Shimla on my first visit, I met Bhisham Sahni, the Hindi novelist, almost daily for three months. He was the Institute's guest. I was genuinely impressed by his humility and dignified reserve. Later I met him whenever I visited Delhi, right until a few months before his death. Once he wrote me a postcard saying that he planned to visit me at Santiniketan. I waited and waited, however Bhisham-ji never appeared. Later he told me that, on his way to me, Aparna Sen had suddenly requested him to play an old Muslim gentleman in her film *Mr and Mrs Iyer*. He did not refuse and gave a memorable performance.

I met some more inspiring people while collecting material. First and foremost I must mention Alex Aronson. A German Jew, he came to Santiniketan in 1937 via London to teach English. He escaped the Nazi butchers staying with Rabindranath Tagore and remained deeply grateful to him and Santiniketan all his life.[7] After the war, Alex left India and settled in Israel. While in Santiniketan he wrote that singularly deft study *Rabindranath through Western Eyes*[8] which has been an inspiration for me to do my historical research. I got in

[7]See Alex Aronson, *Brief Chronicles of the Time*. Writers Workshop, Kolkata 1990.

[8]Alex Aronson, *Rabindranath through Western Eyes*. Kitabistan, Allahabad 1943; republished Riddhi-India, Kolkata 1978.

touch with him to know more, and over a number of years until his death in 1995, we carried on a lively, thought-provoking correspondence. Thrice I met him, once in Stuttgart and twice in Haifa (Israel). We began our correspondence in English because Alex was averse to using the language of the Nazis. When we became attached to each other, he switched to German which, after all, was his mother-tongue. Alex Aronson guided my research, my translation and literary work with his encouragement, praise and affection selflessly. When Visva-Bharati honoured him with its Desikottama in 1993, I felt equally honoured when I was asked to take it to Haifa and present it to him as he felt unable to endure the strain of a trip to India.[9]

Another German-speaking Tagore scholar whom I met was Professor Heinz Mode. When I began my research, Germany was still divided. Mode had been a Tagore scholar in East Germany. He had spent some time in Santiniketan and knew a certain amount of Bengali. His book on Rabindranath was long and rambling and filled with communist clichés. When I visited him in 1988 at his home in Halle, he was already gravely ill and bed-ridden. He probably knew that he had not much longer to live. So he made over to me his entire Tagore library. It contained almost all the books which were written on the Poet and published by the Poet in Germany from 1914 onwards. Heinz Mode had to pull some strings so that the East German government allowed me to take the books with me to the West. My mother sent medicines and toiletry to the Mode household from West to East until Germany united a year later and all necessities were freely available.

The Rabindra-Bhavan archive contains the complete set of letters Rabindranath's German translator, Helene Meyer-Franck wrote to the Poet. They are beautiful, handwritten letters, full of reverence

---

[9]For a summary of his life and work, see Martin Kämpchen, *Alex Aronson: Refugee from Nazi Germany in Santiniketan.* In: *Jewish Exile in India 1933-1945.* Edited by Anil Bhatti and Johannes H. Voigt. Manohar / Max Mueller Bhavan, New Delhi, 1999, p.127-149.

and unction, and give a vivid impression of how Rabindranath was viewed in Germany during the decade of his fame (1921-1930). Obviously, with the exception of a few typescripts, Rabindranath's letters are not contained in the archival file at Santiniketan. Where, then, are they? That was my query. Had they been destroyed during the Second World War? Helene Meyer-Franck and her husband had lived near Hamburg. I asked a friend to look up the archive of Hamburg University. – Nothing! For years I snooped around without getting a clue. The mystery got solved when I contacted Meyer-Franck's publisher, Otto Melchert. Her book of Tagore poetry translations had appeared in Melchert's publishing firm, Deutscher Literatur-Verlag, in 1947. Meanwhile the publishing house had totally changed its profile and had lapsed into irrelevance, but Otto Melchert, deep into his eighties, a tall, unbent gentleman, was still alive.

He ushered me into his office in Hamburg and showed me a portrait of RabindranathTagore hanging at the wall – a treasured picture since decades. Otto Melchert personally kept Rabindranath's letters to Helene Meyer-Franck as well as some related material. He showed the hand-written and typed letters to me. All I asked him for was to yield a xeroxed copy to me which he did without delay and ado. Considering his age, I further implored him to surrender the originals to the Deutsche Literaturarchiv where they would be safely kept and honoured. It needed some prodding and pleading, but after a few months the old man agreed. I informed the director of the manuscript section in the Deutsche Literaturarchiv who personally travelled to Hamburg to accept Rabindranath's letters. Now I could, after a long wait, put the two parts of this correspondence together and have it published [5]. A few months after Otto Melchert had surrendered these letters, he tragically died in a car accident.

Some more original material came into my hands, quite unasked for. I followed various leads with the hope to unearth more and more documents on Rabindranath in Germany. Among others, I contacted the Ecole d'Humanité in Hasliberg Goldern (Switzerland). This private school was founded by the well-known German educator

Paul Geheeb and his wife Edith near Heidelberg. In 1930, on his third and final trip to Germany, Rabindranath visited the school. His erstwhile student in Santiniketan, Aurobindo Bose, had been associated with the school and had requested his master to give the Geheebs the honour of his visit. Rabindranath and Paul Geheeb became quite attached to each other and exchanged letters for a decade.

When Paul Geheeb had to move the school away from Nazi Germany in 1934 to safety in Switzerland, Aurobindo Bose continued to be in touch. He was a journalist for Indian newspapers, a maverick of uncertain occupation during the pre-war and war years and continued to be based at the Ecole d'Humanité until his death. So his papers were left with the school. Much of this material in German or English was absorbed by the school's archive. But what to do with the Bengali letters and manuscripts? – When I arrived to scrutinize the archive for material I might need, Arnim Lüthi, in charge of the archive, asked me whether I was willing to retain these Bengali papers as they were of no use to them. Soon after I agreed, my post-office in Germany delivered a large cardboard box to me. To my surprise and delight, among many irrelevant articles and letters, I discovered over a dozen letters handwritten by RabindranathTagore.

I took them to India in my hand-luggage and went straight to Rabindra-Bhavan in Santiniketan and showed my find to the curator. He flipped through the pages and then put the file back into my hands. "Interesting", he pronounced and turned to other work. Some months later, after he had heard about this faux-pas, the then director of Rabindra-Bhavan, Sankha Ghosh, called me and requested me to let them have these letters. By then, I had decided to present them to the Deutsche Literaturarchiv. This is where they are being kept now, with a German translation and explanatory notes attached, and some pages have already been exhibited in their museum.

No report on my Tagore study is complete without mentioning Professor Prasanta Kumar Paul, Rabindranath's biographer in Bengali. He is the scholar who, over the years, inspired me most in

Santiniketan. Over a stretch of two decades or more he produced nine volumes of biography. Day after day, year after year, he sat at his small desk in a room which should rather be called a monk's cell, and produced one volume after another. The sheer boldness and tenacity of this man! He was, some say, not easy to get along with. He had his angularities. Maybe! But he was, as long as he lived, the one source of inspiration in Santiniketan which kept me going with my translation and my research. I had an easy and amiable relationship with Prasanta-da. When I wrote my short Tagore biography, the only one extant in German [3], he had always time to clear my doubts and provide me with the facts and figures I needed. Never was he in a hurry or impatient. He wrote a long and affectionate preface to my Bengali book [4] and agreed to be the co-editor of the RabindranathTagore – Helene Meyer-Frank Correspondence. Peace be to his soul!

Whoever tries to accomplish something slightly out of the ordinary, should not be surprised at having to face opposition. I wanted a life which questions and tests conventions and follows the path of creative living. I believe a few people doubted my sincerity, especially when they discovered no self-serving reason behind my labours. How can it be that a person spends his life studying and working on Sri Ramakrishna and Rabindranath Tagore? Where does he get his money from? What does he get out of it? I was, and possibly continue to be, a riddle to such people. The same government which had awarded to me the "Rabindra Puraskar" for my work on Rabindranath Tagore in 1992, wanted to throw me out of the country for the identical reason three years later. I was informed that my visa would not be extended. Why? – "He can conduct his Tagore research and translation work just as well in his own country." I flew to Delhi to find support and received it from a highly placed Bengali lady, the daughter of my former landlord at Santiniketan. She talked to the Bihari gentleman in charge of my problem. When I met him, he made some impatient, depreciatory remarks about "those Bengalis" and overruled the order. I re-applied for the extension of my annual visa and returned to Santiniketan, relieved.

But another problem soon cropped up: I could not leave India for my summer sojourn to Germany until my visa application had been granted. This often took many months. I had lectures scheduled with the Indo-German Association in Germany. When I explained my situation to its officials, one phoned up the Indian Ambassador of Germany, who immediately promised me a five-year visa, to be issued from his office. I flew to Germany, went to Bonn, then still the capital, and within a few hours was the jubilant owner of a five-year visa. I could continue my cultural mission and hope to continue it in future.

CHAPTER 2

Rabindranath Tagore in Germany

If I were asked who was the greatest poet India has produced, including the greatest of ancient India, Kalidasa, my firm answer would be: 'Tagore' ... It is tragic, however, that his greatness as a poet will never be generally acknowledged, like the greatness of Goethe, Hugo or Tolstoy.[10]

These two sentences by the well-known writer Nirad Chaudhuri who was born in what today is Bangladesh, sum up the fate of Rabindranath Tagore as a literary figure. On the one hand, they emphasize the immense importance his work receives in West Bengal and Bangladesh; on the other hand, they clearly demonstrate the limit of his importance. Tagore's direct influence does not transcend the confines of the Bengali language. Bengali is spoken by approximately 180 million people in West Bengal and Bangladesh. This is a larger figure than the entire German-speaking population. Yet, Bengali is considered a regional language of the Indian subcontinent (with a limited significance even within the context of the subcontinent), whereas German is accepted as a world language, as indeed many European languages are. We are all aware of the political and economic history which

[10]Nirad Chaudhuri: *Thy Hand, Great Anarch! India 1921-1952.* Chatto & Windus, London 1987, p.596.

created such an imbalance between the languages and the cultures in the world.

Congenial translations needed

Hence it entirely depends on the availability of congenial translations whether Rabindranath Tagore's true worth will be appreciated beyond Bengal. Making Shakespeare, Dante or Tolstoy one's own with the assistance of excellent translations is comparatively easy. Shakespeare can be translated, and is being translated, for the last two hundred years into German with immense success. But translating Tagore into German does not merely entail two neighbouring European languages, but two languages which are divided by separate cultures, social and religious contexts and by geography. He who wants to translate a poem by Tagore from Bengali to German needs to bridge that gulf which separates India and Germany.

It is not easy for an Indian or a Bangladeshi to admit that their national poet, Rabindranath Tagore, is little known in Germany. For Bengalis, Rabindranath Tagore continues to have a powerful, sometimes overbearing, cultural presence. It is virtually impossible to ignore him, even though one may reject him. For Germans, however, Tagore represents the memory of a Wise Old Man from the East who arrived in Germany after the First World War to dispense consolation and courage to a people in a spiritual and cultural crisis. For about a decade, Tagore enthused German audiences and readers, after which he sank into oblivion, a process which was aided by the advent of Nazi Germany for which the Indian poet was anathema.

The mystical atmosphere of Tagore's poems and his lyrical prose has enthralled European readers for several decades. These poems were rendered into English by the poet himself and then translated into German. Tagore's own English renderings may be considered paraphrases. He transformed his finely chiselled verses into rhythmical English prose often simplifying the content by leaving out some of the more complex ideas and evocations, or by adding new imagery. It is however universally agreed that, whatever be the inherent worth of these English texts, they do not echo the intricacy, vigour and musicality of Tagore's original poetry.

If we examine the kind of poems Tagore selected for translation, we realize that they were predominantly his "spiritual", "mystical" poems. He must have presumed that they especially appeal to Western readers, and he was not mistaken. But in the bargain, Tagore sacrificed a large spectrum of his themes, styles and moods which he did not present to the non-Bengali public. His selection of poems helped to reinforce the image of Tagore as a mystic.

Rabindranath Tagore's visits to Germany

In 1921, Rabindranath Tagore visited Germany for the first time. The German people had just suffered a humiliating defeat in the First World War. Burdened with the crushing demands made by the Versailles Treaty, they longed for a "saviour" who could re-establish their self-esteem and help them find meaning in life again. Before entering Germany, Tagore expressed that he empathized with the German people in their hour of crisis and that he had come to strengthen her. Tagore mesmerized his German audiences. Wherever he spoke, the halls were packed. Indeed, the newspapers reported scuffles and regular fights by people who were refused entry. The German press rose to the occasion by reporting Tagore's every movement. He was fêted as the Wise Man from the East, the Prophet, the Mystic.

Tagore's poetry had a direct appeal to Germans of that generation because it had a romantic flair and was imbued with spiritual idealism – and yet, in all its strangeness it was still easily accessible. His poetry embodied a religious imagery, essentially Vaishnava in character, which was innovative for Western ears. To them, this culture of feeling was unfamiliar in its directness, its eroticism and involvement with nature and the cosmos – and yet, the poetry was totally comprehensible. Tagore himself, attired in his long dark gown and with his white flowing beard and serene face, radiated a certain erotic energy.

Tagore revisited Germany in 1926 and 1930. Although the early biographies of Tagore characterize Tagore's three visits to Germany as unmitigated success stories, Tagore himself preferred to take a more detached view. In 1921, he wrote to a friend:

> It has been a wonderful experience in this country for me! Such fame as I have got I cannot take at all seriously. It is too readily given, and too immediately. It has not had the perspective of time. And this is why I feel frightened and tired at it and even sad.[11]

The German-speaking press was by no means unanimous in its praise. There were three major points around which the criticism of the press revolved:

(1) Tagore, a Hindu, wanted to influence Christians in their faith and ultimately convert them to Hinduism.

(2) German writers deserved a slice of the Indian writer's enormous fame, as they were no less talented and relevant in their writing.

(3) Tagore's seeming "oriental lethargy", "bloodlessness", "Indian mildness" was inimical to German or European "dynamism", to its "action-oriented" mindset. It was felt that this European mindset was desperately needed to support the reconstruction of the German nation after the First World War.

Rainer Maria Rilke, Stefan Zweig, Thomas Mann and Hermann Hesse

The adulation Tagore received from the masses rather deterred serious German fellow writers from making an evaluation of Tagore's literary merit. They even shied away from meeting him. Yet, there were two of Germany's eminent contemporary writers who met Tagore and two others who took a serious interest in him and acclaimed him as a figure of consequence.

[11]*Rabindranath Tagore: Letter to a Friend.* Edited by C.F.Andrews. Macmillan, New York 1929, p.171.

Let me first turn to *Rainer Maria Rilke* (1875-1926). Even a few months before Tagore was awarded the Nobel Prize, Rilke recognized Tagore's importance which he expressed in a letter to Lou Andreas-Salomé.[12] Rilke had heard another famous writer, the Frenchman André Gide, read out his French translation of *Gitanjali* which had impressed Rilke considerably. Further, Rilke mentioned his praise of Tagore in a letter to the German publisher Kurt Wolff.[13] At the time, Wolff had just secured the English manuscript of *Gitanjali* for his publishing firm and it was already being translated. Quick to see his advantage, Wolff offered to Rilke that he translate *Gitanjali* into German, as Gide did into French. Rilke considered the offer deeply for some time and then rejected it. This is the explanation he gave in his letter to Kurt Wolff:

> *I do not find within myself that irrefutable call for the proposed assignment, from which alone could emerge a definitive and responsible work. Although much in these stanzas has a familiar ring, it seems, so to speak, to be borne towards me on a tide of unfamiliarity... This may be partly due to my meagre acquaintance with the English language.*[14]

Rilke is not known to have commented on Rabindranath Tagore thereafter, not even in 1921 when the latter was in the zenith of his fame.

Stefan Zweig (1881-1941), the Austrian writer, and Thomas Mann were introduced to Rabindranath Tagore in the summer of 1921. True to their temperament, their reactions to Tagore were quite opposite to each other. Zweig, the suave cosmopolitan and altruistic humanitarian, had visited India in 1908/09. He was appalled by the poverty and misery and later bemoaned the feeling of

---

[12]See Rainer Maria Rilke – Lou Andreas Salomé: *Briefwechsel.* Edited by Ernst Pfeiffer. Insel Verlag, Frankfurt 1975, p.300 (dated 20th September 1913).

[13]See Kurt Wolff: *Briefwechsel eines Verlegers 1911-1963.* Edited by Bernhard Zeller and Ellen Otten. Verlag Heinrich Scheffler, Frankfurt 1966, p.136f.

[14]Op.cit., p.138f.

"insurmountable unfamiliarity"[15] that overcame him when he faced India's tumultuous life. Yet, he maintained an active interest in India's freedom struggle and in her intellectual life. He also observed Rabindranath's rise to fame in Europe and exchanged views on him with that other European intellectual with a keenly critical and supportive interest in India, Romain Rolland. So when Kurt Wolff informed Stefan Zweig that Tagore was to change trains in Salzburg en route to Vienna, Zweig who resided in Salzburg, jumped at the chance to meet him. The short meeting was meaningful to Zweig. Returning home, he immediately penned a letter to Wolff in which he wrote:

> *Thank you very much for the information regarding Tagore's travel programme. This enabled me to spend half an hour in his company today at Salzburg railway station while he changed trains. Thanks to you, I have encountered this great personality, of whom I formed a strong and profound impression.*[16]

Zweig continued to observe Tagore's impact on the European public. Zweig unequivocally appreciated Tagore's message of humanism, while he was critical of Tagore's ostensible penchant to seek publicity. When Tagore chose to visit the philosopher Count Hermann Keyserling in Darmstadt for a week, Zweig commented that Tagore "was unwise enough to have his visit publicly announced"[17]. And in 1926, Zweig criticized Tagore for this "new mania of travelling around Europe as a missionary of the spirit" which he calls a "contagious disease"[18].

Thomas Mann (1875-1955) was both less sympathetic and more complex in his reaction to Tagore. Initially, he even refused to meet

---

[15]Stefan Zweig: Benares: Die Stadt der tausend Tempel. In: Zweig: *Begegnungen mit Menschen, Büchern, Städten.* S. Fischer Verlag, Berlin/ Franklfurt 1956, p.260.

[16]Kurt Wolff: *Briefwechsel eines Verlegers.* p. 414

[17]Romain Rolland – Stefan Zweig: *Ein Briefwechsel 1910-1940.* 1st vol. 1910-1923. Verlag Rütten & Loening, Berlin 1987, p.640f.

[18]Rolland – Zweig: *Briefwechsel.* 2nd vol. 1924-1940. p.187.

him. In 1921, Mann was approached by Count Hermann Keyserling to write an essay on Tagore which was meant to publicize the "Tagore-Week" Keyserling planned in Darmstadt. Mann refused and was also unwilling to go and attend Tagore's lectures. In a letter typical of Thomas Mann, he explained the reasons for his negative response:

> *Dear and Respected Count Keyserling,*
>
> *I cordially thank you for your letter. It exudes so much enthusiasm that I almost packed my bags and went to Darmstadt. However this would have been easier than writing an article, particularly one canvassing for the famous Indian of whom I have, whether you believe it or not, no understanding, or almost none, until now. [...] The image I have always had of him is picturesque but pallid. Surely I do him an injustice in assuming that the subjective pallor of this image reflects reality; in presuming him to be a typical Indian pacifist, animated by a somewhat anaemic humanitarian spirit and a mildness which I deemed almost hostile in the years I spent engrossed in violent emotional conflict. Surely the man is totally different. Since I understand from your letter that he has made a deep impression on you, he must be great.*[19]

Thomas Mann alluded to the well-known duality between European strength and Indian "pallor", "mildness" to which he gave a distinctly negative connotation. The letter was cleverly crafted. Mann had his say on Tagore clearly and then made a rhetorical volte-face by declaring: "Surely the man is totally different. Since [...] he has made a deep impression on you, he must be great." In this manner, he could pronounce his reservations and still hope not to offend the famous Count.

A few weeks later, however, Thomas Mann was unable to avoid coming face to face with the "pallid" Indian poet. Mann lived in Munich and Tagore arrived in that city for several lecture engagements. Tagore delivered a lecture at the University, and on

---

[19]Thomas Mann: *Briefe 1889-1936*. Edited by Erika Mann. S. Fischer Verlag, Frankfurt 1961, p.188f.

the next day Kurt Wolff, Tagore's German publisher, invited some people from the intellectual élite to a reception at his home. Thomas Mann and his wife Katja attended both the lecture and the reception. Mann noted down in his diary the impressions of this second day:

> *At 11 drove with K[atja] to K. Wolff's for R. Tagore's lecture. Select gathering. The impression of a fine old English lady gained strength. His son was brown and muscular – a masculine type. I was introduced, said 'it was so beautiful' and pushed K. forward: 'my wife who speaks english better than I'. He did not seem to grasp who I was.*[20]

What had happened? Tagore's long robe and his flowing hair had reminded Mann of a "fine old English lady" which was a rather rude remark. When Mann was introduced to Tagore, he avoided a conversation by pushing his wife forward and claiming that she speaks English better than he and hence should be spoken to. After thus studiously avoiding contact with Tagore, Mann should not have been too surprised that the poet did not recognize his German colleague, the famous Thomas Mann. Yet Mann's pride must have been bruised.

Hermann Hesse (1877-1962) never met Rabindranath Tagore although one would have expected him, more than anybody else, to seek and maintain a contact with the Indian poet. Hesse had been involved with Indian philosophical thought since his childhood. His parents were Protestant Christian missionaries in South India. His maternal grandfather, Heinrich Gundert, had been a pioneering scholar of the Malayalam language and culture. Hesse, like others in his time, naïvely conceived of India as a country of spiritual perfection and angelic human beings. This romantic notion was bound to be shattered when Hesse set out on his one long trip outside Europe which took him to Sri Lanka and Indonesia in 1911. He was unable to set foot on mainland India as, due to illness, his trip had to be cut short. But he witnessed Hindu and Buddhist culture.

---

[20]Thomas Mann: *Tagebücher 1918-1921*. Edited by Peter de Mendelssohn. S.Fischer Verlag, Frankfurt 1979, p.529f.

Hesse was disillusioned with Asia, but then his expectations had not been realistic. He published his diary notes and returned to his experience again and again in letters, short stories and essays. Slowly, his disappointment transformed itself into a new vision of India which was less idealistic. Formerly, Hesse had believed in the dichotomy of the "spiritual East" and the "materialistic West". Now he chose to perceive an undercurrent of mysticism in both East and West. He envisioned a spiritual unity encompassing both.

The best-known result of Hesse's Indian experience is his "Indian novel" *Siddhartha.* When Rabindranath Tagore toured Europe in 1921, Hesse was deeply involved in writing this novel of an Indian spiritual aspirant's path to fulfilment. He lived in the Ticino mountains in southern Switzerland almost like a hermit. The idea of travelling to Germany or Austria to meet Tagore must have been far from his mind. And yet, Hermann Hesse kept an eye on the intellectual developments of his time. He reviewed three books by Tagore (*Gitanjali, The Gardener* and *The Home and the World*) and expressed his views in several letters. The last letter in which Hesse referred to Tagore is from 1957. Hesse was not fascinated by Tagore to the same degree as were Stefan Zweig, Romain Rolland and Hermann Keyserling. Strangely, Hesse considered Tagore's writing as too European and not of exceptionally high quality, although he did laud the nobility and dream-like beauty of his texts. Hesse did however fully support *The Home and the World* concluding his review with the words: "[...] the more people read this book the better."[21]

In his last letter, Hesse commented on Tagore's "partial eclipse in the West" after the Second World War. Hesse opined that Tagore had been "a fashion" in the 1920s and now had to pay the price for being out of fashion. Yet, in some minds and hearts the effects [of reading Tagore] have lived on and borne fruit, and this continuing influence – impersonal, silent and in no way dependent on fame

[21]Vivos Voco (Leipzig), vol. 1, Nov. 1920, p.817.

and fashion – may in the final analysis be more appropriate to an Indian sage than fame or personality cults.[22]

Rabindranath Tagore in Germany Today

We return to the question of translations. Translations of Tagore's works into German started to appear from 1914 in rapid succession. No sooner did they come out in London, were they taken up by Kurt Wolff. Already in 1921, an eight-volume *Collected Works* could be published to coincide with Tagore's first visit to Germany. When the devaluation of the German currency began in 1923, the entire book market began to collapse. Kurt Wolff continued to publish new volumes of translation until 1925, and then he had to stop. In 1929, his firm went bankrupt. There were several persons who had prepared translations of Tagore's works for Kurt Wolff. From among them Helene Meyer-Franck was the most dedicated and diligent. From 1918, she became the sole translator of Tagore into German. Her husband, Heinrich Meyer-Benfey, and she brought out his *Collected Works*.

After Kurt Wolff's publishing house collapsed, a new phase began for Helene Meyer-Franck. She learnt Bengali for the sole purpose of reading Tagore, her "dear Master", in the original. It was a lonely fight in her small town near Hamburg, as she was virtually on her own. However, she learnt to read Bengali sufficiently well to translate into German three novellas and a collection of poetry. The novellas were published as early as 1930, but they left no visible traces because of the Nazi Reich which emerged in 1933. Helene Meyer-Franck had to wait until after the Second World War before she was able to publish the second slim volume. Soon thereafter first her husband and then she died. As a result, her initiative to translate Tagore directly from Bengali was not being emulated and continued. In the 1950s, the old translations from English, published between 1914 and

[22]Hermann Hesse: Preface. In: *Later Poems of Tagore*. Translated and with an introduction by Aurobindo Bose. Peter Owen, London 1974, p.7.

1925, were republished in West Germany, and in some cases new translations of these weak and flawed English texts came out.

Communist East Germany had a special relationship with Tagore. The latter's internationalism endeared him to the regime, and his work was given weight. Tagore's books were translated into German in much larger numbers than in the West. Yet, these translations were, generally, of doubtful quality. Several anthologies contained translations from the English and from the Bengali side by side; other books were translated via Russian. Then there were so-called team-translations, i.e. a Bengali knowing little German and a German knowing little or no Bengali teamed up to produce a translation. None of these methods was satisfactory, and they did not serve to enhance Tagore's reputation as a figure of World Literature. As far as I can see, only one person in erstwhile East Germany mastered Bengali well enough to produce a competent translation on her own; that was Gisela Leiste, who translated the novel *Gora.*

It was not until the 1980s and 1990s that fresh direct translations of Tagore's poetry were brought out, first by Alokeranjan Dasgupta in collaboration with Lothar Lutze (one volume) and then by Martin Kämpchen (six volumes). I believe that in Germany Tagore's time has now arrived. Apart from the fact that any great literature has a claim to be noticed and respected throughout the world simply because it is great literature, I wish to identify three areas in which Tagore's ideas and ideals have a strong relevance for us today:

(a) Ecology. – Rabindranath Tagore's love of nature was inspired by the awareness that all living beings, including animals, trees and plants, are endowed with a soul. On this level human beings are equal with "low" creatures and plants. We are all co-creatures of God's creation. Accordingly, Tagore's praise and worship of nature is born of a deep spirit of togetherness and feeling of a creational bond between humans and nature. Such a sense of unity is missing in modern Western ecology. It emphasizes the usefulness of nature and the necessity of a natural environment for the practical survival of mankind. Thus, with his poetry and his essays, Tagore can inspire a deeper understanding of and togetherness with the natural environment.

(b) Education. – Rabindranath Tagore's ideas of education continue to be relevant. He wanted to unfold the entire personality through music, songs, dance, theatre, art, contemplation of nature, meditation and social service. The Indian subcontinent has strayed from these ideals, and in Western countries, too, the demons of "usefulness" and "efficiency" have to be tamed by the purpose-free, playful activity of Tagorean education.

(c) International understanding. – Rabindranath Tagore's deep yearning for harmony among men, achieved through mutual tolerance and asceticism, is as worthy of imitation now as it was then. It is not enough to nourish dreams and circulate hopes. Tagore has demonstrated to us how much *one* inspired human being is capable of achieving among men. Tagore ascended from his dreams into reality and worked out understanding between human beings gradually.

CHAPTER 3

Rabindranath Tagore's Integration into European Culture

Carl Zuckmayer, one of Germany's leading playwrights of the 20th century, a former assistant to Bertolt Brecht in Berlin, told a touching story about Rabindranath Tagore. Zuckmayer wrote it for the International Literary Seminar in New Delhi in November 1961, Tagore's birth centenary year. Zückmayer narrated the following significant episode:

> *Let me begin with a little story from the First World War in which I took part as a young German soldier. A friend of mine who was a sergeant in the medical corps told it to me. To the front hospital in which he worked as an assistant surgeon they brought one day an Indian soldier who had been taken prisoner after he was badly wounded in both legs. There was no other chance to save his life than an immediate amputation of one of his legs. But for this purpose the chief surgeon wanted the consent or at least the confidence of the wounded man. The Indian soldier who served with a "Gurkha-Regiment" in the British army spoke no German, of course, and his English was rather unintelligible. Moreover, the German medical officers knew little English. So there was almost no chance for mutual understanding, and the more they tried, the more our poor Indian soldier grew fearful and anxious. God knows what he had been told before about the cruelty of the enemies, for*

he believed that they were going to kill him or do to him some other serious harm. It was then that my friend [...] thought of the only Indian word, or name, he knew – it was the name of the Indian poet [...] Rabindranath Tagore. So he bent down his head to the Indian who lay in the cold sweat of fear and whispered in his ear this name: Rabindranath Tagore! Rabindranath Tagore! Rabindranath Tagore! After he had said it three times the Indian seemed to understand. His face relaxed, a shy little smile came into his eyes, then he closed them, his fear was gone, and he nodded weakly his consent and confidence to the enemy doctors.[23]

Carl Zuckmayer continues:

I felt touched by this unpretentious little story – for it seemed to me to hold a peculiar significance: what a name, a single name, can mean as a bridge of understanding and faith between men. I don't mean "a name" in the superficial sense of fame, reputation, publicity. I mean the magic of a name – a name as the expression and the symbol of a personality bearing and spreading the token of universal ideas through our world. I don't think that my friend the medical sergeant had known much more than the name of Rabindranath Tagore, and I doubt if the Indian soldier knew more about him. But in this name there was the seed of good will, of reconciliation, of faith and hope. [24]

Before discussing Carl Zuckmayer's story, I add another episode, this time from the Second World War. It happened in Warsaw, the capital of Poland. The Jews lived in the infamous Warsaw Ghetto in inhuman conditions, constantly threatened by extermination. Janusz Korczak was a physician and a writer of considerable reputation. A believing Jew, he was dedicated to the welfare of orphan children for whom he had built an orphanage home in 1910. When the Jewish ghetto was established by the Nazi invaders, Janusz Korczak

---

[23]Carl Zuckmayer, *Rabindranath and Germany*. [Proceedings of the] International Literary Seminar, Sahitya Akademi, New Delhi 11.-14. 11. 1961 [cyclostyled], p. 1f.
[24]op.cit. p.2.

could have arranged to escape, after all he was a famous citizen who could demand certain privileges. Instead, he chose to stay behind with his children. He tried to rescue them, but all he could do, was to prolong their lives for some weeks or months. When the Warsaw Ghetto was dissolved in August 1942, Korczak and his children were deported to the notorious concentration camp of Treblinka. He lead his band of two hundred small children, a green flag in hand, to the railway station where they were pushed into cattle wagons heading for Treblinka. They all perished.

Only a few weeks earlier, in July 1942, inspired by Janusz Korczak, these orphans gave a performance of Rabindranath's *Dakghar* (*The Post Office*) in Polish translation. A contemporary eye witness describes this performance thus:

> *The children of the Orphanage identified with the character and image of Amal who appeared to them as the rainbow on a cloudy day and avidly absorbed each word that came out of his mouth. These children were suffocating within the ghetto walls and would desperately peer into an opening in the wall to see what was happening on the 'other' side... With bated breath they awaited, together with Amal, the king's letter that would spell redemption. Amal believed and anticipating his own rescue fell into a sweet sleep.*[25]

Another surviving eye-witness called the performance of *The Post-Office* in the Warsaw Ghetto "a heart-rending experience, the like of which could never be seen again". When after the performance Janusz Korczak was asked why he chose this particular play, he said that "eventually one had to learn to accept serenely the angel of death"[26]. In other words, he and the children were prepared by the play and its comforting portrayal of death for their own great challenge of accepting death.

---

[25]Janusz Korczak, *The Ghetto Years 1939-1942*. Ghetto Fighters' House [Tel Aviv 1980], S. 80.

[26]Bruno Bettelheim, *Recollections and Reflections*. Thames and Hudson, London 1990, p. 206.

Both episodes, the one related by Carl Zuckmayer featuring the First World War, and the one happening in the Warsaw Ghetto of the Second World War – reveal a deep penetration of Rabindranath's poetic world into European culture. At the point of death – that is, at a time of absolute crisis – only that which has a total subjective meaning to our own life will be remembered and invoked. The German soldier invoked the name of "Rabindranath Tagore" to inspire confidence in the wounded Indian soldier who feared for his life. Korczak invoked the indomitable love of freedom in his death-bound orphan children, expressed by the death-bound boy Amal. Here the words of a poet rise above the cultural context and above the point of history in which his words were born. They become directly applicable to a human situation and respond to it existentially by offering meaning and consolation.

What does Europe know of Rabindranath Tagore?

By quoting two striking examples of Rabindranath making an existential difference in the European context, I do not claim that Tagore was broadly accepted or was fully known for what he is. After receiving the Nobel Prize in 1913 for the one slim book that was published in English, *Gitanjali,* one translation after another appeared in English in quick succession, some translated by the Poet himself, others by his associates in Santiniketan. But this accounts for just a few percent of his Collected Works – the *Rabindra Racanabali* – which runs into 18 large tomes in Bengali (in the Visva-Bharati edition) and still does not collect all Tagore has published and written during the eighty years of his life. Hence, in India we have the curious situation that the "national poet", the one writer of India who received the Nobel Prize of Literature, cannot be read fully and in the original by her peoples save the population of West Bengal. It documents the predicament of a nation which is proud of her linguistic plurality and multi-ethnicity.

German translation of Rabindranath Tagore began almost as early as English translation. While the English *Gitanjali* appeared in 1912 in London, the German *Gitanjali* followed in 1914. Yet, these two translation ventures have a totally different cultural significance. In Great Britain Rabindranath was a poet from the colonies using the language of the colonizers who succeeded in expressing himself on the sophisticated level of literature. It was like beating the political adversary with his own weapons. Or, viewed from the opposite angle, it was the peak of success after one hundred years of British education in India.

In Germany, the German translation carried no such ideological and political signal. In Germany, Rabindranath was not the poet of a colonized nation speaking to the colonizers; rather, he was a voice from the "mystic east" speaking to the mysticism- and mysteries-seeking West. He was seen in the tradition of German Indology which began in the early 19th century simultaneously with German Romanticism. German Romanticism had discovered India as a land of philosophy and wisdom. Hence, the German public of the early 20th century saw in Rabindranath an exponent of the philosophy and wisdom of India – not so much a literary figure, not a poet. This is the clear message we get after reading the German newspaper articles written on Tagore during his visits to Germany. More importantly, the sympathetic German public saw in Tagore a fellow-Romantic and considered his Romanticism as the entry point through which to understand and appreciate him. Tagore was probably aware of this tradition as he, on a number of occasions, stressed the special cultural link between India and Germany.

Similarly, *Gitanjali* was not so much considered to be poetry and literature in Germany than texts for philosophical inspiration. The question of translation – its accuracy and cultural problematic – was entirely neglected in the public debate about Tagore. However, a few writers, especially Rainer Maria Rilke and Thomas Mann, who had a deeper perspective did point out that Tagore's English was not his mother-tongue. Even the admirable correspondence between Rabindranath Tagore and his principal German translator, Helene Meyer-Franck, never discussed points of translation. It was quietly taken for granted that since Rabindranath wrote in English, a European language, the transfer to German, another European language, was smooth. It did not enter the mind of the public that Rabindranath's mother tongue was non-European, that he perhaps thought and felt in his own language which in turn would affect the characteristic shape and sound of his English.

In the important first decade of Rabindranath's exposure to German readers, from 1914 to 1925, one book after another was translated from English to German in rapid succession. In all, not less than 27 books came out within that period of eleven years. [See 7] Rabindranath's visit to Germany in 1921 greatly enhanced the sales. Hence, it was possible that an eight-volume *Collected Works*[27] was published at the end of that year, making it the first Collected Works of Tagore outside Bengal. Kurt Wolff, Rabindranath's ambitious and business-minded publisher, arrogated to himself a monopoly on the Nobel Prize winning poet. He did not allow any other publisher and no translators not connected with him, to take up new translations, even though the existing translators were, for several years, unable to cope with the demand for new books. However, quite a number of short texts came out, translated by different hands, in journals and magazines; some even tried to mould the English prose into German verse.

The first three German books that came out, all of them in 1914, were translated by three different persons[28]. Three more translators[29] were employed until 1918, before Helene Meyer-Franck entered the scene with her translation of *Der Geist Japans.* In 1919, one additional translator[30] had his debut, but from 1920 Helene Meyer-Franck reigned as the only translator until the final translation, *Gora,* which came out in 1925 in two volumes. Helene Meyer-Franck was

---

[27]Rabindranath Tagore, *Gesammelte Werke.* 8 volumes. Edited by Heinrich Meyer-Benfey and Helene Meyer-Franck. Kurt Wolff Verlag, München 1921.

[28]Elisabeth Wolff-Merck (Kurt Wolff's wife), Hans Effenberger and Marie Luise Gothein who translated *Gitanjali.*

[29]Annemarie von Puttkamer, Hedwig Lachmann and Gustav Landauer.

[30]Emil Engelhardt.

not only Rabindranath's busiest and most devoted translator, she also carried on a correspondence with Rabindranath for 18 years.[31]

No new translation could be published after 1925, although Rabindranath visited Germany twice thereafter, namely in 1926 and 1930. The reasons are not far to seek. One, a galloping inflation pushed the price of every-day commodities to astronomical heights; books could no longer be easily produced or bought. Two, the Kurt Wolff Verlag declined and, in 1929, it relinquished business. Three, the *Tagore-Rummel*, the "craze" to read, see, touch Tagore was on the wane, and the price Rabindranath had to pay for this exaggerated popularity, was an almost total oblivion soon thereafter. This is how Hermann Hesse viewed it in retrospect:

> *Today's man of fame falls into oblivion after his death, and only after a lapse of time – sometimes prolonged – does the world take the trouble to re-examine and reappraise both his former fame and his present neglect. [...] This is the state of Tagore's reputation in the West today.*[32]

From 1925 until after the Second World War only one more book appeared. That was the translation from Bengali to German of three stories by Rabindranath Tagore. The translator was no other than Helene Meyer-Franck herself. After the enormous popularity of the Indian poet had declined and his sales become a trickle, his publisher, Kurt Wolff, turned away from him. But not so Helene Meyer-Franck. After she no longer received English books by Tagore to translate, she decided to learn Bengali. She and her scholarly husband even wanted to abandon their respective jobs – she was a school-teacher, he a University teacher – and migrate to Santiniketan to live there with Tagore and become useful to his school and University. Elaborate plans to shift their huge library to Santiniketan were made.

---

[31] *My dear Master. Correspondence of Helene Meyer-Franck / Heinrich Meyer-Benfey and Rabindranath Tagore.* Edited by Martin Kämpchen and Prasanta Kumar Paul. Visva-Bharati, Kolkata (2nd ed.) 2010.

[32] Quoted in *Rabindranath Tagore and Germany: A Documentation.* Edited by Martin Kämpchen, Max Mueller Bhavan, Calcutta 1991, p. 43.

While a fair number of European scholars followed Tagore's invitation to spend a year or a few months at his university, Visva-Bharati, Helene Meyer-Franck and her husband were the only Europeans who actually wanted to shift to Santiniketan to stay there for life. However, the British government barred them from entering India.

So with the help of Bengali students and some books, they both learnt Bengali for several years in Germany. It must have been a grueling effort learning Bengali practically all by oneself with only far-away Rabindranath to encourage them by letter from time to time. However, Helene Meyer-Franck became sufficiently competent to translate, from Bengali, three stories which came out around 1930.

Helene Meyer-Franck tried her hand at poetry translation as well. However, with the Hitler regime bringing about cultural fanaticism, Tagore became anathema in Germany, and Meyer-Franck was unable to publish her slim volume of poetry translations, *Mit meinen Liedern hab ich dich gesucht*[33], until 1946, after the Second World War. Meanwhile she sent these translations to Rabindranath who accepted them graciously, but obviously he could not understand them. He passed them on to a German teacher of Visva-Bharati, the then Brahmachari Govinda who later became famous as a Buddhist preceptor and writer under the name Lama Anagarika Govinda. He praised her translations fulsomely saying that they did not read like translations at all.[34]

My own evaluation is that even though these translations sound beautiful, they are too "free" to be called philologically valid. However, they do attempt to create a new German poem which is a huge step forward compared to the lyrical prose that existed so far. Unfortunately, Helene Meyer-Franck's slim book has created no impact. So instead of the path she had shown, namely to go for direct translation, from the 1950s onwards a West German publisher, Hyperion-Verlag, brought out the old translations of Kurt Wolff

---

[33]Deutscher Literatur-Verlag Otto Melchert, Hamburg 1946.

[34]See *My dear Master*, p. 143.

Verlag one by one as well as a few new translations, from existing English versions, with slightly modernized German.

How to make Tagore known in Germany?

Tagore has always been ambivalent about his usage of the English language. He began to gather courage to speak to foreign audiences in English only a year before he was awarded the Nobel Prize. His English *Gitanjali*-renderings may have been, secretly or unconsciously, done with a view of having them published. But in public, Tagore claimed that they had been done as a whim, a recreation when he was weak and ailing. The Nobel Prize gave him the audacity to produce one English paraphrase of his Bengali books after another, without, often, ascertaining its standard. In his later life, Tagore bitterly regretted that he had rushed into this translation work caring too little for the quality and genuineness of the results. His letters to William Rothenstein, his British friend, bear this out. Although Tagore became immensely popular, especially in England and in Germany, these philologically rather inadequate translations have affected the image Tagore received and the literary weight he was accorded outside India until the present time. His popularity was too effortlessly gained and was predominantly built on his personality and his ideas, less on his literary works.

When we read press articles from Europe of the 1920s, we realise the attraction Tagore exerted on the masses as a person. Tagore is not entirely above suspicion of encouraging this kind of image. Certainly his fancy oriental gown, his flowing beard and Sufi cap helped him in creating a style for himself from which the imagination of the naïve European audiences took off to create their own romanticising and sentimentalising fantasies. In other words, Tagore was, at that level, entirely *un*integrated into the European cultural context. In fact, for effect he relied on being exotically different, rather than attempting an integration into European culture.

That Tagore "pose" stood in the way of integrating him into European culture for several decades. People who attend my lectures on and poetry readings of Tagore in Germany and Austria are mostly elderly and expect to become spiritually edified. The audience is surprised when I tell it that I do not wish to emphasise Tagore the Mystic, but Tagore the Poet and the Man of Literature.

Tagore's own translations have prevented the realisation that his works are not properly represented by them. The general feeling has been that since the poet himself had translated his works into English, these translations must be authentic. Hence, fresh translations from the original Bengali took a long time to take shape. As for English, translations have been continuously attempted by associates of the Poet for the benefit of non-Bengali Indian readers and for the British public. They were published specially in the English-language journals of Visva-Bharati and by the Visva-Bharati Publishing Department (Granthan Vibhag). Looking at these translations it is striking to notice that they do not make an attempt at fashioning a proper English poem from the original Bengali text. Even such prestigious publications as *One Hundred and One Poems by Rabindranath Tagore*, edited by Humayun Kabir in 1966[35], in which many leading Bengali intellectuals translated their favourite poem, do not produce successful poems in English translation. There seemed to be an inherent conviction that Tagore cannot be fully and genuinely translated into English. Hence tedious summaries and entirely unpoetic prose renderings of the surface ideas were all that was attempted.

In Germany, the situation was different, but equally uninspiring. The old translations published by the Kurt Wolff Verlag disappeared from the market after the economic depression forced the publishing firm to liquidate in 1929. These translations were all from the English versions fashioned by Tagore and his friends. During the Nazi period from 1933 to 1945, Tagore was a non-entity in Germany. No books by him were published, nor was he discussed in journals.

---

[35]Rabindranath Tagore, *One Hundred and One Poems*. Ed. by Humayun Kabir, Asia Publishing House, Bombay 1966.

Only after 1945, Rabindranath Tagore witnessed a gradual resurrection. As mentioned, first, the old German translations were republished and new translations were made from Tagore's English versions in a slightly modernised German. Then communist East Germany (GDR) took up the promotion of Tagore's works and brought out several works in direct translation from Bengali on the occasion of Rabindranath Tagore's birth centenary in 1961. The East German publisher, Verlag Volk und Welt, was more inventive and explorative than West Germany. It is easy to see why East Germany should have had a special interest in Tagore. The Indian poet was an "internationalist". With his typical idealism he advocated the understanding between nations, peoples and religions. He believed in the power of love not only between individuals, but between groups and nations. This poetic project of international understanding appealed to the communist ideology of brotherhood among nations.

However, the books that came out in East Germany were not yet as editorially balanced and philologically mature as they should have been. The publisher brought out a four-volume *Selected Works of Rabindranath Tagore* with two novels, several novellas and short stories. While Gisela Leiste translated *Gora* from Bengali (keeping the Russian translation close at hand), *Chokher Bali* was translated from the English version, *Eyesore*. The novellas were partly translated from English by a German and partly by a Bengali from the original. The same confusion was created in the volume of short stories. Naturally, the Bengali spoke little German and the German translator little or no Bengali. So, it was like the lame leading the blind. One anthology by the name *Kabuliwallah, O Kabuliwallah*[36] inadvertently translated the same poem twice – once from the Bengali original in *Sisu,* and again from Tagore's English translation, *The Crescent Moon.*

It took another two to three decades until *philologically correct* as well as *poetically relevant direct translations* began to appear. In

[36]Rabindranath Tagore, *Kabuliwallah, O Kabuliwallah.* Stories, aphorisms and poems. Edited by Karlernst Ziem, Alfred Holz Verlag, [East-]Berlin 1961.

England it was William Radice's book *Selected Poems of Rabindranath Tagore*, published in 1985, which set a clear signal for such demanding translations. Although slovenly translations have appeared since then which imply that it is enough that a poem's surface content of facts and ideas is conveyed, these books were punished by being ignored. Other books with translations of a high standard do emerge, for example Ketaki Kushari Dyson's *I Won't Let You Go* (1991) and the *Oxford Tagore Series* edited by Sukanta Chaudhuri for the Oxford University Press which can be placed side by side with William Radice's efforts.

In Germany, it was Alokeranjan Dasgupta who with Lothar Lutze, his erstwhile professor colleague at the University of Heidelberg, brought out a small volume of late poems by Rabindranath in 1987. The book's title *Der andere Tagore* (*The Other Tagore*) announced its "programme" and intention. Dasgupta and Lutze wanted to portray not the Wise Man and Mystic, not the poet of quaint lyrical images which seem to evaporate when you study their literary substance. Instead, they looked at the existentially questioning, probing, deeply troubled poems of the last ten to fifteen years of his life. It placed before the German-speaking audience a man and poet who had no similarity with the person and the work they had known through his publications in the early twentieth century.

My own efforts followed in the footsteps of William Radice whose translations inspired me and served me as a model, although my selection was quite different from his. Radice does not shy away from supplying copious notes on each poem he translates. Each poem is briefly introduced, then a line-by-line commentary follows which clarifies the meaning wherever necessary and points out complexities in the translation. Quite naturally, a poem is a poem and should be appreciated without notes and commentaries. This is, for example, Lothar Lutze's and Alokeranjan Dasgupta's viewpoint who furnish hardly any aids for comprehension in their book. I, instead, hold the view that a poem which has to travel from an Indian language to a European language, from one culture to another, from one religion, one social background, one emotional context to another – and not merely from one neighbouring language to another, as for example in the case of German and English or German and French – then a *mere* translation, no matter how competent, does not suffice! Hence, when we translate Tagore's Bengali poems into English or German, too little of the substance of the poem can be retrieved in a translation. Notes must supplement the translation. They provide, as it were, the subtext to the poem introducing us to the context within which it was written. This is indeed a controversial decision, but I stand by it.

In 1990, I brought out the volume *Wo Freude ihre Feste feiert* [9], containing fifty poems and songs by Rabindranath Tagore in my translation, with introductory notes and a line-by-line commentary. These poems are a cross-section of Tagore's poems and songs starting with very early ones and concluding with the stark, brief poems he wrote on his deathbed. My talent intuitively reaches out to melodious, song-like poems or songs proper with a strong emotional impact. So such poems represented the majority.

Already a year earlier, I had published a selection of Rabindranath's aphorisms [8]. A third book of translation, *Am Ufer der Stille*[10], appeared in 1995 with a fine selection of photographs on Santiniketan and its rural landscapes (by Samiran Nandy).

If I wanted to integrate Tagore into the German cultural context, I would have to go beyond translation. So I wrote the first biography of Tagore in German [3] (which is in its third edition). And I researched on Tagore's relationship with Germany, especially on his three trips to Germany during which he made contact with numerous writers and scholars of repute. This research was made known in my three books on the subject (all published in English in India) [1, 5, 6]. Thus a framework was created with the help of which I hope for a deeper appreciation of the poet in Germany.

These three volumes of poetry translation mentioned earlier were all brought out by publishers specialising in religious books. At the time it was impossible to find a good *literary* publisher. Tagore's Wise Man-image attracted German publishers of religious books and rather discouraged publishers of literature. For a full decade I tried to place Rabindranath Tagore's poetry into the context where it belongs, namely with a mainstream publisher of world literature. This wish was fulfilled in 2004 when the German publisher Insel Verlag in Frankfurt brought out a selection of Tagore's *Love Poetry* [11] in my translation. Insel is a large, traditional literary publisher. A year later, in 2005, I brought out a 670-page volume of *Collected Works* [12] containing chapters with selections of poems and songs, two plays, two short stories, essays from Bengali and from English, letters and conversations with Albert Einstein. The publisher, Verlag Artemis & Winkler, has brought it out in their series "Winkler Weltliteratur" (Winkler World Literature). The translations are carefully introduced and annotated in a commentary section of 130 pages. This German book has lifted Rabindranath Tagore out of the mould of the mystic poet and presents him as a figure of world literature.

Theatre as a Medium of Integration

I can think of several areas where Rabindranath Tagore could find a place in modern European life. For example, the contemporary concern for the environment could be deepened and made spiritual through Tagore's celebration of nature. Further, his internationalism could, now that the East-West division of political ideologies no longer exists, receive a fresh meaning and importance. Here, however, I want to emphasise the European stage as the medium through which Tagore's works and ideas can penetrate European consciousness and be absorbed by it. The stage seems to be an especially suitable forum to achieve an integration into the texture of modern European culture. Stage-craft transforms a text on several levels and with the help of different media – like music, stage props, costumes, style of presentation – into a different, new whole.

Let me give you two examples of a dramatic text written by Tagore which was wholly transformed and integrated into European cultural expressions without, I believe, losing its Indian or "Rabindric" soul.

The first example is, again, *The Post-Office* (*Dakghar*). This play holds a profound attraction for me, so I translated it into German. Translating the *Sri Sri Ramakrishna Kathamrita* (*The Gospel of Sri Ramakrishna*) from Bengali to German had sharpened my skill in handling colloquial dialogue. The important task was to make Amal's conversation sound effortlessly simple. It should have none of the laboured pompousness of the original English translation. This natural, vibrant simplicity evokes all the layers of meaning there are in this play. I realised that, of all of Tagore's plays, *The Post-Office* can be most easily adapted to the European stage because it has no songs, no mythological allusions, no complicated subplots referring to social problems in India. It is as timeless, and yet it is as contemporary, as are modern European existential theatre plays, for example Samuel Beckett's *Waiting for Godot.*

The German theatre director Wolfram Mehring read my translation and put *The Post-Office* on stage in Switzerland. From old photos we know that when Tagore directed the play in Kolkata, the stage props were full of allusions to Indian reality (thatched hut, Indian costumes etc.). Mr Mehring discarded all cultural references to India. He even knowingly "Germanised" the pronunciation of the characters' names. He carried his drive for abstraction so far as to ban all stage props and to stylise the dialogue and the actors' body movements in order to allow the play to unfold its internal allegorical content clearly.

Later, the play was taken up again, interestingly, by a Swiss school for handicapped children. These handicapped children acting out *The Post-Office,* some in wheel chairs, could profoundly empathise with Amal's illness and find solace in his defiant zest for life and in his peaceful transition from sleep to death. The idea of these children performing *The Post-Office* is not dissimilar to the motives of the death-bound children at the Warsaw Ghetto putting up the play. In recent years, my translation was produced as a puppet play in the municipal theatre of Magdeburg (in erstwhile East Germany) and was kept on the repertoire for several seasons.

Another of Tagore's allegories was put on stage in recent years, that is the long narrative poem *Devoured by the Gods* (*Debatar Gras*)[37]. The Indian composer Param Vir, born in 1952 in Delhi, who has made England his home and was educated according to the western musical tradition. He chose this poem as the plot for an opera. William Radice wrote the opera's libretto. Although keeping within the frame of a modern western orchestra, Param Vir nonetheless kept emotionally close to Indian themes. In the case of the opera *Snatched by the Gods*, the combination of an Indian composer working in the Western musical tradition and an Englishman with an affinity to Bengali culture has again demonstrated the fertility of such cross-cultural creative efforts. In our time of easy and swift communication between people and cultures, these cross-cultural creative efforts are the sign of our epoch.

By writing the libretto of *Snatched by the Gods*, Radice faced the enormous challenge of transposing (in his own words) the "dramatic and emotional perfection of Tagore's poem" into a dramatic dialogue which "worked" on the stage. Not only this, the ballad's distinctly Indian background and content had to be universalised; or, to put it more clearly, their "Indianness" had to be abstracted and the plot and meaning of the story expressed in symbolic terms which were comprehensible universally. As a result, the opera is still located on the Ganga, the characters are still pilgrims travelling to the mouth of the Ganga for a sacred bath and then back home. But no further reference is made to the Hindu tradition of pilgrimage, to bathing at auspicious moments, to the sanctity of the Ganga, and to the superstition which leads to the sacrifice of the boy Rakhal.

The realisation that superstition can occur not only within Hinduism but in any religion with similar destructive results helps us to see the plot as an archetypal battle between the subconscious forces of light and darkness, between the persecutor and the persecuted, between the heroic rescuer and the dumb fear of the masses. Within this

[37]Published in William Radice's *Rabindranath Tagore: Selected Poems* (p.62-66).

framework Rakhal is idealised as the "true pilgrim who seeks the freedom to realise himself" (as Param Vir writes). Rakhal is the innocent, blameless "sacrificial lamb". In the extreme crisis of the life-threatening storm on the river, these forces within man are manifested and acted out with a brutal immediacy, that is, without the softening guise of social convention.

The opera *Snatched by the Gods* had its premier show in May 1992 at the Munich Biennale, which is an "International Festival for New Music Theatre". The orchestra and its conductor were from Amsterdam, while most of the singers, as well as the director, were British. In the premier show Rakhal was sung by a gifted Indian boy living in Britain.

The music is strongly impressionistic and imitates sounds in an onomatopoetic fashion, a feature which recommends itself in this drama full of storm, winds and high waves. Yet, the music is far from being simply naturalistic. The music also works out the emotional stirrings of each character in fine nuances. Often the pilgrims sing in a chorus or in overlapping lines to bring the friction and tension between them to an almost physically painful climax. One would have to listen to the music several times with complete attention to grasp the intricate patterns of the music.

On the stage in Munich there was neither boat nor river. True to the archetypal character of the plot, there was only a platform suspended low from the roof which the actor-singers rocked to and fro to indicate the movement of the boat in the restless waves. The ankle-deep black sand spread evenly on the entire stage was soon covered with deep foot-prints, with troughs and mounds from the movement of the actor-singers. This soon strongly symbolised the emotional commotion of the persons involved in the drama.

With this opera we witness an exemplary process of integration into European culture: Tagore's original Bengali narrative poem has first been translated into English, then transformed into another literary genre, a drama. It was finally set to music in the European opera tradition and put on stage following the aesthetic sensibilities of young, modern Europeans. For once, that is, Rabindranath is not the exotic Wise Man, not one who is too far removed from one's own cultural bearings to be relevant to contemporary European life. It is Rabindranath Tagore minus his sombre dark cloak, a Rabindranath who, variously transformed and reincarnated, is vibrantly alive within the texture of European culture.

But is it still Tagore at all? – Yes, I do think so. The basic thrust of his narrative poem, *Debatar Gras*, remains intact. That is, the author's disdain for superstition, his condemnation of cruelty and insensitivity in the disguise of piety. William Radice writes aptly that for him the opera was a "deeper and richer 'translation' of the Bengali poem" than he had ever thought possible. It may in fact be argued that after the cultural specifics have been abandoned, the poem has revealed an additional dimension of meaning which earlier readers in India were not aware of.

For a full integration of Rabindranath into contemporary European culture similar efforts will be welcome. Why not set more and more Rabindranath's songs to Western music as had been done in the first half of the twentieth century? Why not adapt other plays or narrative plots for the European stage? If courage and creative energy are not lacking, there are limitless possibilities.

The Other Tagore

For a creative genius like Rabindranath Tagore to mutate into various literary genres and artistic expressions comes quite naturally. He has written poems which he later set to music and formed them into songs. While waiting for the right phrase to occur to his mind, he began to scribble on his manuscript pages; this then slowly evolved into doodles and in bizarre, grotesque figures. This was the beginning of Tagore's career as a *painter* which began when he was already almost sixty years of age. The doodles migrated as full images on to canvas. In 1930, he mounted a number of exhibitions in Europe and in the USA, so also in Berlin, Dresden and Munich. These paintings ran counter to his image as a poet of an idealistic philosophy and a high-minded social agenda. In his paintings Tagore was down to earth, funny, extravagant, expressionistic. His subconscious mind surfaced reveling with abandon in its visions and illusions. Tagore allowed it to happen naturally. Put into historical perspective, with these paintings Tagore became the founder of modern Indian art.

In Santiniketan, Tagore had, in 1901, settled to begin a school according to the ancient *brahmacarya asrama* model. He referred back to traditional Hinduism in order to develop a modern alternative to the soulless British school-system which he detested since he himself had been a victim of it as a boy. The Ashram teachers and students stay together as in a family. The teachers are meant to be living examples to their pupils in all matters of daily life. They do not only teach in classrooms and from books, but they are meant to inspire and motivate. Every Ashram has a "guru" who in Santiniketan was Rabindranath Tagore himself. He wanted his students to learn through his songs and poems, by enacting his plays and music dramas, by visiting the peasants in the surrounding villages and by observing and celebrating nature. Here again, Tagore's songs and plays mutated into pedagogical tools for the emotional and intellectual evolvement of young minds. Tagore himself sang his songs and acted in his plays on stage besides working with his students on his plays as their director. He easily slipped in and out of various roles, each of which needed its own definitive talent.

Tagore's constantly creative mind knew no rest even when he was fatigued and sick. He had to express his every mood while on his sickbed, while feeling the pangs of old age and approaching death. He had no hesitation to reveal his fear, his anxiety, and his desperation, going against his image as the poet of spiritual joy, of romantic yearning and beauty.

In Rabindranath Tagore we have, perhaps for the last time, a man of universal creative genius who knew to express himself in every literary genre as well as in music, art and pedagogy. He, in his age, was still able to bring together the human sciences and the natural sciences into one unified vision of life. Afterwards such a vision would break down into the "Two Cultures" theory with the humanities and the natural sciences following their separate paths of acquiring knowledge and making it applicable to modern life. Although efforts are being made to again unify these two cultures, perhaps each of them is by now too diversified and specialized to be understood by one single mind.

In Rabindranath Tagore, finally, we still have the idealistic effort to visualize the "east" and the "west" as one global whole, as "world culture". Today, such a vision would be rejected as, at best, naïve. Globalization is a concept of technology, of commerce, of communication. Globalized culture would need to follow the diktat of economic strength and thus probably lose its specificity and become irrelevant to the needs and visions of human beings who are, as they should be, rooted in a culture defined by time and space.

Books referred to in the text

On Rabindranath Tagore

(1) *Rabindranath Tagore and Germany: A Documentation.* Max Mueller Bhavan (Goethe-Institut), Calcutta 1991, 160pp. [Tagore's contacts with German writers and scholars]

(2) *Rabindranath Thakur O Jarmani: Ekti Lekhyayan.* Translated by Sardar Abdus Sattar & Naseem Akhter Hussain Ghas Phul Nadi Publication, Dhaka (Bangladesh) 1998, 160pp. [Bengali edition of the previous book]

(3) *Rabindranath Tagore.* Bildmonographie. Rowohlt Verlag, Reinbek 1992, 3rd edition. 2002, 160pp. [German Biography of Rabindranath Tagore]

(4) *Jarmanite Rabindra-Biksha.* Translated from the English by Jaykrishna Kayal. Mitra & Ghosh, Calcutta 1999, 187pp. [In Bengali: Tagore Studies in Germany]

(5) *My Dear Master. Rabindranath Tagore and Helene Meyer-Franck / Heinrich Meyer-Benfey. Correspondence 1920-1938.*

(Co-edited with Prasanta Kumar Paul), Rabindra-Bhavana, Visva-Bharati, Santiniketan 1999, 141pp.; 2nd revised edition Visva-Bharati, Kolkata 2010, 144pp.] [Correspondence between Tagore and his German translator, with introductions and notes]

(6) *Rabindranath Tagore in Germany: Four Responses to a Cultural Icon*. Indian Institute of Advanced Study, Shimla 1999, 128pp. [Tagore's relationship with Hermann Keyserling, Kurt Wolff, Helene Meyer-Franck and Heinrich Meyer-Benfey]

(7) *Rabindranath Tagore and Germany: A Bibliography*. Rabindra-Bhavana, Visva-Bharati, Santiniketan 1997, 80pp. [Bibliography of books and contributions in journals by Tagore and on Tagore from 1913 to 1997, with Index]

Translation of Tagore poems from Bengali to German

(8) *Rabindranath Tagore – Auf des Funkens Spitzen*. Selected, translated from the Bengali and introduced. Kösel Verlag, München 1989, 3rd enlarged edition 1997, 127pp. [Aphorisms from *Lekhan, Kanika* and *Sphulinga* by Tagore; with photographs. Dutch edition: 1991]

(9) *Rabindranath Tagore – Wo Freude ihre Feste feiert. Gedichte und Lieder*. Selected, translated from the Bengali and introduced. Verlag Herder (Herder Taschenbuch 1684), Freiburg 1990, 189pp. [Fifty poems and songs by Tagore, selected from his earliest until his late poems]

(10) *Rabindranath Tagore – Am Ufer der Stille*. Selected, translated from the Bengali and introduced. Benziger Verlag, Düsseldorf 1995; new editions 2002 and 2008, 102pp. [Poems and songs by Tagore, with two essays on Tagore. With photographs by Samiran Nandy.]

(11) *Rabindranath Tagore – Liebesgedichte*. Selected, translated from the Bengali and introduced. Insel Verlag (Insel

Taschenbuch 2988), Frankfurt 2004, 3rd edition 2006, 105pp. [Love poems of Tagore]

(12) *Rabindranath Tagore – Das goldene Boot. Lyrik, Prosa, Dramen.* Selected, translated from Bengali and English with introductions and notes. Verlag Artemis & Winkler (Winklers Weltliteratur), Düsseldorf 2005, 669 pp. [edition of Tagore's works comprising poetry, short stories, one novel, plays, essays, letters and his conversations with Albert Einstein; edited by Martin Kämpchen, translated by Rahul Peter Das, Alokeranjan Dasgupta, Hans Harder, Martin Kämpchen, Lothar Lutze, Andor Orand Carius, Axel Monte]

Bio-data

Dietmar Rothermund
Satinder Kumar Lambah
Martin Kämpchen

Dietmar Rothermund, Ph.D. FRHistS,

Professor emeritus of South Asian History, South Asia Institute of Heidelberg University.

Born in Kassel, Germany, 20 January 1933. Married to Chitra née Apte, three children.

Studied history and philosophy at Marburg and Munich universities 1953-56 and at the University of Pennsylvania, Philadelphia, 1956-59 (Ph.D. 1959). Research Fellow of the German Research Council in India, 1960-62. Visiting Fellow, Australian National University, Canberra 1962. Junior staff member, South Asia Institute 1963-67, Habilitation in Modern History 1967, Professor 1968-2001. Fellow of the Royal Historical Society, London, since 1988. Honorary member of Humboldt University, Berlin, since 1994. Chairman, European Association for South Asian Studies 1997-2008. Member of the Indo-German Consultative Group 1992-2002 (nominated by the German Foreign Office).

Recent Publications: *India: The Rise of an Asian Giant*, New Haven and London: Yale University Press 2008, (with Hermann Kulke) *A History of India*, 5th ed., London: Routledge 2010, *Gandhi und Nehru: Zwei Gesichter Indiens*, Stuttgart: Kohlhammer Verlag 2010.

Satinder Kumar Lambah

Satinder Kumar Lambah was born in Peshawar (now in Pakistan) on July 16, 1941. He holds a master's in history from St. Stephen's College, University of Delhi. He joined the Indian Foreign Service in 1964. Over a diplomatic career spanning more than four decades of experience of working in several Indian mission across the globe, Satinder K Lambah has also held the important posts of Ambassador of India in Hungary (1986-89); High Commissioner of India to Pakistan (1992-95); Ambassador of India to Germany (1995-98); Ambassador of India to the Russian Federation (1998-2001). He was Deputy Secretary General of the 7th Non Aligned Summit held in Delhi in 1983 and later Coordinator of the Commonwealth Heads of Governments meeting in India. His specialization has been in dealing with India's neighbours.

After retirement from the India Foreign Service in August 2001, he chaired a Committee on the Reorganisation of the Ministry of External Affairs and India's Missions Abroad. From November 2001 to July 2002, he was India's special envoy for Afghanistan. During 2004-05 he was the Convener of the National Security Advisory Board (NSAB) Government of India. At present he is Special Envoy in the Office of the Prime Minister of India. He was also elected President of Federation of Indo-German Societies in India. During his tenure as Consul General of India in San Francisco (1989-91) he was conferred a "Trustees' Citation" by the University of California, Berkeley in 1991 for his initiating, coordinating, and spearheading the campaign which generated over US$2 million in a short span of four months for Indian Studies, resulting in the creation of two Chairs of India Studies, a bi-annual lecture by a distinguished scholar from India, and an annual scholarship at the Graduate School of Journalism at U.C Berkeley. He is married to Nilima Lambah, author of "A Life Across Three Continents – Recollections of a Diplomat's Wife". They have two children.

Martin Kämpchen

Born on 9th December 1948 in Boppard (Germany), Martin Kämpchen did his Primary and High School education in his home-town. He earned a one-year scholarship to be an exchange student at an American High School in 1965-66. He attended the University of Vienna (Austria) and the Sorbonne of Paris (France) studying German Literature, Philosophy, European Theatre and French. He completed his studies in 1973 with a Ph.D. in German Literature from Vienna.

Martin Kämpchen visited India for three months on a German Government travel grant in 1971. From April 1973 to 1976, Kämpchen was a lecturer of German at the Ramakrishna Mission Institute of Culture in Calcutta. During these years he lived at the Ramakrishna Mission Ashram of Narendrapur. He went back to

University in 1977 at Madras (Chennai) doing an M.A. in Indian Philosophy, and at Visva-Bharati University, Santiniketan, where he completed a Ph.D. in Comparative Religion in 1987 on a comparison of Sri Ramakrishna and Francis of Assisi. He lives in Santiniketan since 1980.

While returning to University in 1977, Kämpchen turned to freelance writing as a profession. As a journalist he focusses on topics related to Indian culture, especially her literatures and religions. He contributes to journals and to the radio. He has also worked as the cultural correspondent for the German national daily *Frankfurter Allgemeine Zeitung* for 15 years. He has translated the *Sri Sri Ramakrishna Kathamrita,* Ramakrishna's conversations with his disciples, and the poetry of Rabindranath Tagore.

Kämpchen has written and edited several books on Christian-Hindu dialogue and on Indo-German cultural contacts in the 20th century. In addition, he has written four volumes of short stories mostly on Indian rural life. A novel has been published in 1999.

Since the early 1980s, Kämpchen has done social work in two Santal (Adivasi) villages 10 km from Santiniketan, in Ghosaldanga and Bishnubati, where he has helped to build up several educational institutions, medical, agricultural and economic programmes. He has been instrumental in fostering Santal culture accompanying cultural groups to many places in India, to Bangladesh and five times to Germany and Austria. The Santal-medium school is recognised as a model effort, equally the museum of Santal Culture in Bishnubati.

Scheduled to be published in 2011 on the occasion of Rabindranath Tagore's 150th birthday:

(1) *Rabindranath Tagore – Gedichte und Lieder*. Selected, translated from the Bengali and introduced. Insel Verlag, Berlin 2011 [Translation of approx. 70 new poems from Bengali to German]

(2) *Rabindranath Tagore und Deutschland.* Deutsches Literaturarchiv (Marbacher Magazin 134), Marbach 2011 [Tagore's contacts with German writers and scholars; in German language]

(3) *Mein lieber Meister. Rabindranath Tagore und Helene Meyer-Franck.* Draupadi Verlag, Heidelberg 2011 [German translation of "My dear Master"]